Outsider art

Roger Cardinal

Outsider Art

WITHDRAWN

Studio Vista London

© Roger Cardinal 1972
Published by Studio Vista
Blue Star House, Highgate Hill, London N19

Set in 11/12pt Monophoto Baskerville 169
Photoset by BAS Printers Limited, Wallop, Hampshire
Printed in Italy by Alfieri and Lacroix S.p.A.

ISBN 0 289 70168 6

Contents

1 Towards an alternative art

The characteristic property of an inventive art is that it
bears no resemblance to art as it is generally recognized
and in consequence—and this all the more so as it is
more inventive—that it does not seem like art at all.

Jean Dubuffet

Cultural conditioning

In our specific historical and cultural situation, we look out upon a particular range of works grouped under the heading of Art. The welter of monographs and art histories, the relative frequency and variety of exhibitions, public concern about the running of national galleries, these are obvious confirmation of a conception of Art as a publicly honoured domain where some of the most signal achievements that make man most deeply aware of his superiority in the animal kingdom are assured a lasting place. The great works of the past—the Rembrandts, the Raphaels, the Velazquez, the Da Vincis—are confirmed masterpieces in the Western tradition. The great works of our times—the Braques, the Moores, the Vasarelys—are, we feel certain, bound for consecration in the same annals. One has only to glimpse at the concluding paragraphs of the most respected and most monumental Histories of Art in order to hear that hum of authorized satisfaction that constitutes the basic note in the repertoire of Cultural Man. To such a man, it would be inconceivable that the history of art could be in any real sense revolutionized. True, its stresses can be modified, as the works of forgotten masters are from time to time reassessed and placed higher on the scale; fads have their day, and yesterday's 'way out' avant-garde settles into its ordained historical niche. But nothing really changes: Great Art continues to last. Inasmuch as we are all affected by the culture in which we are brought up, it seems idle to consider any benefit in posing the simple question: 'is this all?' And yet this question raises a whole gamut of issues, involving all kinds of cultural, social, indeed psychological prejudices. It is the aim of this book to raise this question and thus to take issue with these prejudices. The challenge to be faced is this: can art be conceived that is not 'cultural'? Does such a rigorously *different* art exist?

In his pamphlet *Asphyxiante culture*, a classic statement of an anti-cultural attitude, the artist Jean Dubuffet relates an instructive anecdote to illustrate the degree to which cultural preconceptions can completely stifle the proper apprehension of anything that resists accepted ideas about art. It concerns a conversation he had with a teacher to whom he tried to expound the hypothesis that throughout history there have always been forms of art alien to established culture and which *ipso facto* have been neglected and finally lost without trace. The teacher expressed his conviction that if such works had been assessed by contemporary experts and deemed unworthy of preservation, it was to be concluded that they could not have been of comparable value to the works of their time that had survived. To support this view, he cited the example of some German paintings he had seen in an exhibition. Though these had been executed at precisely the time the impressionist school was directing art into new channels, they bore no traces of that influence. After submitting these forgotten works to a thorough and objective perusal, the teacher felt obliged to admit that they were aesthetically inferior to the work of the impressionists; art criticism had accordingly been perfectly justified in preferring the latter.

Dubuffet points out the stupidity of this sort of reasoning, based as it is on a notion of objective value that betrays the worst kind of cultural myopia: where respected critics have testified their approval, there can be no dissension; bad marks in art can never be forgiven, at least not by the layman. Dubuffet stresses the futility of the man's 'objective' certainty, and suggests that it is only as a result of a particular education, of a particular cultural formation that the teacher made the judgement he did. His aesthetic preference was totally determined by these factors. A difference in his background, or a difference in the opinion of the experts might well have led to a completely different assessment of the paintings concerned. Instead, the teacher bowed before the prevailing wind emitted by the Establishment, and could consent to find objective beauty only in the place marked out by a superior order.

In *Asphyxiante culture*, which appeared in 1968, a year when all aspects of French life were being vigorously questioned, Dubuffet is reacting against a specific notion of culture obtaining in a state which has its official Ministry of Culture exerting control over the populace through the Maisons de culture which it has set up in most large towns, and an educational system firmly backed by a heritage of failproof masterpieces. The issues Dubuffet raises are nonetheless of relevance to the whole of Western culture, for it might indeed be surmised that cultural indoctrination is no less strong in other countries for being organized on less overt lines.

Cultural conditioning is such, says Dubuffet, that nobody dares dispute the value of a play by Racine or a painting by Raphael, those who have no direct acquaintance with these works being often the most ardent defenders of their supposed value. In this way Cultural Man has conceded whole tracts of his mind to the imprint of stereotyped opinions and evaluations about which no doubt may be voiced. There may be intellectuals and teachers, Dubuffet concedes, who cannot stand Racine. But they do not quite dare to say so, for they have an uneasy feeling that the pricking of one myth might set off a chain reaction in which they would forfeit all their prestige. Rather than risk uncontrollable revolution, they content themselves with a mediocre revisionism and, for example, proudly place 'subversive' books written half a century ago on the high school curriculum.

Thus nothing changes very much in the eyes of Cultural Man: even the myth of progress is an established museum-piece. Every minor novelty takes its place in a system so well organized that it has a high tolerance even to heresy. All avant-garde revolutions in art turn into history: the slap in the face of culture given by Dada has now been framed and hung on the museum wall.

It is this museum wall, which one may imagine lined with purple velvet, that may be thought of as the symbol of cultural impregnability. Here is where all will hang who have, perhaps despite themselves, allowed official culture to take them for its own. It is highly significant that when Dubuffet asked the teacher to imagine works of art that had failed to prevail against the dictates of taste laid down by the higher representatives of culture, the latter at once thought of pictures he had seen *in a museum*. His mind, suggests Dubuffet, was incapable of conceiving of pictures as existing elsewhere than in a museum. For him pictures that do not hang on museum walls do not deserve any consideration, and certainly cannot be called *art*. Thus it is that no alternative location of art, no location outside the approved areas of museum, gallery or so-called 'private collections' assumed to belong to rich connoisseurs, is conceivable. For Cultural Man, art is the monopoly of the privileged intellectual and the professional artist, and though art does spill over into daily life in the form of municipal exhibitions, discussion in the public media, newspaper reports about the sums paid when masterpieces change hands, the art system is sustained at the centre by a cultural ideal that is untouchable and inalterable, based as it is on the unshakeable belief in such things as 'our cultural heritage', 'the legacy of the past' and the fetish of the 'great masterpiece'.

The sense of a glorious continuum, of a 'history of art' in which man has progressed triumphantly from mastering the technique of painting on the walls of caves to that of producing silk-screen prints, ignores the fact that true art history is in fact a succession of revolts and heresies. Over all dissension, though, an academic standard has tended to prevail, whereby all that purported to be art had to conform to certain fundamental principles. While matters of technique or subject have varied over the centuries, one characteristic principle has held sway for a long while, that art has in some sense to aspire to beauty, beauty as defined, of course, by the cultural mandarins. Academic art, art which is fabricated to an agreed formula of beauty, always seems of a piece, being sustained by unwavering loyalty to the Graeco-Roman heritage and by concepts like proportion, harmony, healthiness. It is exactly in defiance of this uniform standard that the authentic discoveries have been made and movements like romanticism and expressionism have arisen—though even such as these have been assimilated as being interesting 'freak' moments in the glorious history of culture, or else forgotten, by common consent.

Cultural standards cannot be forgotten, since they are safeguarded jealously by the machinery of education. Academic artists are trained to copy the work of the past so as to preserve a continuity. But their work, which survives in the great houses and palaces, is nothing more than a mummified version of art. Academic art is technically 'correct': academic artists 'know how', but do they *know*? The least original mode of expression is to copy what is already there, whether it be another work or an aspect of the external world, naturalistically treated. There is, writes Dubuffet, no mental *depth* about the work of artists whose work is deemed worthy of cultural recognition. It has no real range, and despite a superficial glitter of diversity, is in truth barren and uniform.

These remarks apply not just to the academicism of an earlier age that lingers on in the works of landscape- and portrait-painters in the Royal Academy tradition. For the new academicism has shifted ground somewhat so as to accommodate the modern taste for novelty; it appears in a new guise in modernist, Pop and abstract art, especially of the type which, being polished, clean and inoffensive, perfectly qualifies for official admiration under the established rules that sanction only what Wolfgang Rothe has called 'beauty-without-wrinkles'. Though supposedly at a premium, originality is so rarely recognized that the new academicism tends, like the old, to re-route artists with new ideas across the same old paths. A depressing uniformity of touch is the result: the latest works, applauded in all the right reviews according to a common sense of value that comes as second nature to critics of established status, seem all to be painted by the same hand. In a sense, they have all been painted by the hand of the Culturally Acceptable Artist, who alone knows how to make a Thing of Beauty. But beauty is a myth whose basis is as arbitrary as are the conventions of cultural art at large, a secretion that has grown and been succoured by accidents that have hardened into traditions. If beauty is so central to the present cultural ideal, what should one look for if one is trying to find an alternative art? Not mere ugliness, not the miserable art such as serves the propagandistic ends of social realism. The proper alternative to the cold frisson of beauty must be the feverish spell cast by disturbing, alien works.

Of course it must be acknowledged that all those who live in a given society must to some degree submit to the *Kulturzwang*, the cultural determinism operative upon their milieu. The psychiatrist Leo Navratil points out that while cultural pressure upon man tends to induce a speeding-up of the intellectual capacities, there can be a corresponding slowing-down in the maturation of the personality, and possibly a very real loss in outer and inner freedom. The implications for the artist are exemplified in Navratil's reference to the well-known stylistic contrast between the art of the Neo-paleolithic cave-dweller, who hunted in small groups, and that of Neolithic man living in agricultural communities. The former has a vital realism whereas the latter is schematic and emotionally neutral. The broad distinction is that between the extrovert and the introvert type, between an art springing from a psycho-physical unity to an art affected by the imbalance created by societal pressures.

Since the authentic equilibrium of the cave-dweller is no longer feasible, and since the available cultural art offers only an artificially created balance, it is logical to suppose that an alternative art nowadays must be found in the area of imbalance. Rather than come to terms with the demands of the cultural norm, there do exist artists who have turned away and drawn the essence of their art from this situation of disequilibrium. The purpose of this book is to discuss artists of this strange, non-aligned type.

In posing the question of whether an alternative mode of art is conceivable, I hope to invite the reader to adopt a posture of receptivity towards what is unfamiliar to his experience. Once the question is accepted as a worthwhile one, answers of the sort that I am going to suggest may appear less unacceptable than they might have done at first. I am hoping to persuade the reader that to turn away from habitual cultural patterns to which he has been trained to respond, can be an exciting and an enriching experience, provided the alternative to the old order is not senseless chaos. This remains to be proven: but let us try to proceed on the understanding that the alternative I am positing is not a sombre blind alley. If there is danger inherent in this deviant approach, let me quote the opinion of Anton Ehrenzweig: 'Up to a point any truly creative work involves casting aside sharply crystallized modes of rational thought and image making. To this extent creativity involves self-destruction.' The dangers are the same for both creative artist and committed viewer.

Conditioned as we are, and despite all our best intentions, we cannot hope to sustain a posture of total mobility when it comes to responding to works that escape the old categories. Yet even if we are hampered, not least by the medium of thought which is language, we can at least address our sensibilities to unfamiliar experiences in the hope of gaining some measure of independence from this conditioning. For the function of art when it is genuinely effective, is to give us a chance to break with old habits, and loose the shackles of reasonable social behaviour, the better to retreat down dark passageways and rejoin that part of ourselves which moves towards us with a savage laugh.

In quest of the primitive

Though this book is by no means offered as a history of anti-cultural movements in art, it may serve as a useful preliminary orientation to mention some of the signals of the modern climate in which such a question as 'What else could art be like?' can be raised. One major current of enquiry in this context has been the search for what might in general terms be called primordial artistic expression, the primitive, indeed the savage qualities that make for art that is not subservient to the cultural norm.

In seeking distinctive instances of this kind of search, one can always look further and further back in the history of art. Among the Western artists who first felt drawn towards the virtues of primitivism, many would cite Gauguin, whose journey to the South Seas led to a reanimation of his art; though his artistic training continued to operate, filtering his exotic raw material into refined forms. A more important moment came in 1907, the year that Picasso discovered Negro and Polynesian art. The rhythmic and affective power of these brute representations of the human form were a challenge to the aesthetic ideal of the West. For Picasso however, these works represented an artistic problem to be overcome; and he soon found out how to assimilate the uncompromising 'otherness' of the Negro mask in his painterly transcriptions. He demonstrated to the satisfaction of the guardians of culture that one did not need to consider the tribal function nor the pre-conscious imaginative origins of such works; it was sufficient to treat them as aesthetic stylizations whose appeal was primarily to the intelligence. The theoretical attitudes of cubism diverted primitive intensity into the safe channels of rational analysis and objective description. The same sort of operation was carried out on the 'primitive' work of the fauvist painters. What Marcel Brion calls the 'primeval freshness' and the 'brutal frankness' of these 'wild beasts' of art succeeded in affecting the public only for the short period in which red trees and green faces remained shocking, and before everyone learnt that it was easy enough to cope with these aberrations by talking sagely about 'the problem of plastic form envisaged solely as one of pictorial values'.

A more impressive movement of revolt against the supremacy of the intellectual approach was that of German expressionism, which sought to effect a more than formal deliverance from the comfortable aestheticism and shabby conventions fostered by the humanistic bourgeois culture of the nineteenth century. In a time of social alienation, artists of a highly pronounced individualistic type such as Barlach, Nolde and Kirchner (who responded strongly to Negro masks) worked with anarchistic rage to externalize their visions of a tortured reality, all the while violating the principles of composition and of artistic good behaviour. Though the anguished immediacy of Expressionism has now been damped down by the historicizing process, helped along by the coining of the vague term ending in -ism that has ensured the smudging-over of its wild contradictions and its extraordinary multiplicity of individual styles, this movement may be remembered as one of the more authentically anti-cultural manifestations of modern art.

The more recent movement known as abstract expressionism may be cited as the artist's attempt to get back to a primitive relationship with his materials. The action-paintings of Jackson Pollock are an instance of early experiment in inarticulate textures that led to the deliberately 'illegible' art of painters like Wols and Camille Bryen, who sought to underline the non-human aspect of their work. A good deal of counterfeit brutalism has been offered by the abstractionists in recent years, and art critics have had little trouble in coining the necessary neologisms to cope with these additions to the canon. But occasionally one can find evidence of art that is genuinely primitive in the sense that it emerges from the chaotic realm of undifferenti-ation, being released at the near-instinctual or primary levels of creation. One of the roads on this 'journey to the ends of night' leads to the total extinction of the artist's involvement. The principle of non-intervention can mean an almost total ban on skill, control and initiative. In some cases this leads to a sterile absence of art; in others it can lead to creations of considerable attractiveness—though attractive in their proximity to the forms created by that most authentically non-human artist, Nature. The sort of 'molecular' primordiality of some non-figurative art, resembling as it does the worlds revealed by the electro-microscope, represents a regression beyond human instinct to a kind of vegetable or mineral a-consciousness. At this point one may, with Roger Caillois, prefer to seek beauty in actual stones and fossils.

The fascination of sheer brute matter is one of the prime motors of the work of Jean Dubuffet. But though he works with the humblest substances—cubist *papiers collés* seem insufferably coy in comparison to his *texturologies*, with their tar, grit, broken glass, and anthracite, with only the occasional indulgence such as butterfly wings—Dubuffet's art remains undeniably 'human' by virtue of a firm figurative axis. Though his figures invariably suggest the hand of an utterly unskilled person, the ebullience created by the dose of cerebral humour that he manages to inject is such as to awaken a sense of almost aboriginal gaiety. In its way, Dubuffet's unbeautiful art reminds one of the mixture of rich vulgarity and subtle purposefulness that went into the creation of Père Ubu by Alfred Jarry, the master of *décervelage*—de-braining.

Jarry it was who, probably maliciously, helped to launch the innocent Douanier Rousseau on a career in the Parisian art world at the turn of the century, thus contributing to the popularization of *art naïf*, which has since, thanks to the efforts of enthusiasts from Wilhelm Uhde to Anatole Jakovsky, flourished to the point of becoming a minor genre, even a minor industry in its own right. The problem of the authenticity of naïve art will be discussed later; suffice it to say for the moment that the paintings created by untrained artists whose position in society was often obscure and humble suggested to many an innocence and a spontaneity in refreshing contrast to the works produced by painters inculcated with formal techniques, and thus represented an accessible alternative to the less manageable primitivism of African art. For similar reasons, child art was hailed by an artist as distinguished as Kandinsky, who contrasted the 'effect of inner harmony' conveyed by the untrained hand and the pre-rational mentality of the child with the correct but lifeless art of trained academic painters. Yet again art was yearning for that unspoilt sensibility which Baudelaire had spoken so warmly about when he wrote that 'genius is simply childhood recovered at will'.

The wilful recovery of childlike modes of figuration was a vein exploited by Paul Klee, who governed his 'primitive' spontaneity with the resources of a powerful intellect, nourished on the highest fruits of culture. He is not unlike Mirò in the way he developed a personal calligraphy to express the inarticulate; both appear to be as much clever as intuitive, however, and where Werner Haftmann praises Klee for his 'refined childlikeness' one hesitates to use the word 'primitivism'. It must be said that when Hitler inaugurated the House of German Art in 1937, he paid Klee the unwitting compliment of saying that his works looked as if they had been 'produced in some Stone Age ten or twenty thousand years ago'.

Though theoretically committed to the exploration of the deepest creative strata of the mind, surrealist art has not always been as 'primitive' as it hoped to be. Whether some surrealists were too conditioned in the first place to be able truly to escape from the cultural stranglehold; whether they were too sophisticated to permit themselves the more extreme stances of primitivism, and tended to allow the secondary process of controlled elaboration to follow too soon upon the primary process of projecting unconscious forms from within; whether too many major artists in the movement fell prey to the seductions of popular and official recognition;—these questions need not detain us. What is unquestionable is the extreme enthusiasm that has always been evinced in surrealist circles for the artistic products of the madman and the savage: that certain surrealists themselves went mad is less relevant than the fact that surrealism established a particular tone of response to imaginative creations unshaped by external dogma. The primitivism of Oceanic art was especially prized by André Breton, who admired it as being more flamboyant, more explosive than the poised, stylized art of Africa. As for madness, the surrealists saw it as a creative rather than a destructive condition, something more positive than negative. No better demonstration of the surrealist belief in the delirious fecundity of *l'art des fous* can be found than in the text Breton wrote at the time of the foundation of the Compagnie de l'Art Brut in 1948:

> I am not afraid to put forward the idea—paradoxical only at first sight —that the art of those who are nowadays classified as the mentally ill constitutes a reservoir of moral health. Indeed it eludes all that tends to falsify its message and which is of the order of external influences, calculations, success or disappointment in the social sphere, etc. Here the mechanisms of artistic creation are freed of all impediment. By way of an overwhelming dialectical reaction, the fact of internment and the renunciation of all profits as of all vanities, despite the individual suffering these may entail, emerge here as guarantees of that total authenticity which is lacking in all other quarters and for which we thirst more and more each day.

Madness as the most extreme mental attitude may be expected to produce an art whose essence is alien to the established norms of culture. Indeed it constitutes the major area for consideration in the present enquiry into art external to culture; hence the necessity now for a brief survey of the importance given to the art of the insane in this century.

Madness and art

The fascinating richness and power of works of art produced by mad people has to date been made publicly available in only a limited way. The majority of works dealing with art produced by asylum inmates have been written by practising psychiatrists: most of these are concerned with the purely medical aspects of the material and are highly technical. There is however a growing interest in these 'forbidden' products on the part of non-specialists, and psychiatrists themselves are beginning to move out of the resolutely diagnostic posture and to admit the attractiveness of the works of the insane as art in its own right.

Lombroso's study *Genio e follia* (1882) was the first significant study of the relationship between psychic disorders and artistic creativity. However though Lombroso acknowledged that mental patients did produce extraordinary work, his main concern was with investigating the psychopathological aspects of genius. Artists were, he found, ten times more prone to mental disorders than the average man: genius was accordingly to be seen as a type of psychosis. The equation 'genius = madness' passed into common currency with alarming speed, and even now many people imagine that the force of Van Gogh's later works can be explained simply in terms of his mental breakdown. The worst aspect of confusing simplifications of this sort is that they reinforce convention and prejudice, and help the guardians of culture to rule out anything divergent by labelling it 'mad' and therefore 'unhealthy'. Such adjectives came particularly easily to the lips of the cultural guides to the new Germany of the thirties.

But more intelligent research was under way. In a study centred specifically on the art of the mentally ill, *L'Art chez les fous* (1907), Marcel Réja analysed three types of such art: infantile, ornamental, and symbolic, and noted a certain similarity with the products of children and primitives. Though receptive to the artistic qualities of some of the works he studied, Réja felt bound to conclude that there was little to be said for the idea of the madman as genius. Two important monographs pointed in a more hopeful direction. The first was Paul Schilder's *Wahn und Erkenntnis* (1918), in which the author tried to draw decisive parallels between the pictures of his patient G.R. and the experiments of the avant-garde of the time, especially the abstractionist theories being developed by Kandinsky. Both sorts of art concurred in seeking a spiritual meaning behind sense-impressions, and in envisaging painting as the depiction of ideas. Wolfgang Rothe has pointed out how Schilder's argument amounted to a defence of modern art against philistinism, the implication being that if both the art of the insane and that of the nascent expressionist movement were 'mad', they were both equally worthy of attention as art. The second study of an individual case was by the Swiss psychiatrist Dr Walter Morgenthaler, *Ein Geisteskranker als Künstler* (1921), which dealt with the schizophrenic Adolf Wölfli. For the first time a book was devoted to a mentally ill and interned artist whose name was disclosed in full, rather than being reduced to the initials that are still a current medical convention. There were even photographs of Wölfli in the book. Morgenthaler gives a formal description of Wölfli's grandiloquent prose and lyrical writings, his weird musical compositions, and above all of his remarkable pencil drawings. In the endless inspirational flow of these, Morgenthaler sees the elaboration of a kind of private paradise: 'This world formed according to his desires and his deliriums is for him more authentic than the real world.' Marvelling at the way in which formal structures could be seen to emerge from the chaos of a major psychic disturbance, he characterizes these as being formed by restraints gained in the effort to attain psychic stability through artistic creation—art effecting, or at least reflecting, a species of self-therapy. To artistic creativity was thus attributed a normative function. Though circumspect about the use of an aesthetic rather than scientific vocabulary, Morgenthaler manages to convey enthusiasm for the sheer vitality of Wölfli's drawings, and concludes that the man who composed such astonishingly harmonious works merits unreserved recognition as a genuine artist.

The classic book on the art of the mad remains Hans Prinzhorn's *Bildnerei der Geisteskranken*, which appeared in 1922. It was based on material in what probably remains the largest collection of art by mental patients in the world, comprising 5000 works by some 450 individuals. Working at the Heidelberg psychiatric clinic, Prinzhorn had helped build up this collection by soliciting contributions from institutions in all the German-speaking countries, as well as elsewhere. In the days before the idea of art therapy had been accepted by psychiatry, Prinzhorn was able to claim that the collection was almost entirely composed of works carried out spontaneously. Furthermore they were all created by people who were indisputably mad, and who by and large had had no kind of artistic training. These factors made of the Heidelberg collection something uniquely suited to Prinzhorn's purpose. This was to examine as large a range of works as possible in order to establish what was the central process (*Kernvorgang*) that determined artistic expression. The breadth of view was necessary before he could focus upon the psychological roots of the creative instinct. In this search for a kind of essence, he relied ultimately less upon scientific deduction than on intellectual intuition, to which Ernst Kris testily attributes the shakiness of some of his conclusions.

The mass of Prinzhorn's material is by schizophrenics. Despite the factor of doubtful diagnosis in the many cases not directly known to him, he was able to estimate the predominance of schizophrenic work in the collection as being 75 per cent, the other 25 per cent being divided among five other groups—manic-depressives, psychopaths, paralytics, imbeciles, epileptics. Schizophrenics are in any case more numerous than any other type of patient, and it is now universally recognized that they are the most productive in terms of both written and graphic material. There should be no real deformation of truth therefore if generalizations about the art of the insane are henceforth made in respect of schizophrenic art alone.*

Prinzhorn deliberately avoids using the word art (*Kunst*) in his book: he favours the term *Gestaltung* (forming, shaping), and so emphasizes less the 'artistic' product than the psychological process. This stress at once places his book outside a context of aesthetic evaluation.

The book includes some interesting, though not always original remarks about the expressive urge, seen as a mysterious self-preoccupied drive towards psychic expression; the urge to play (*Spieltrieb*), the decorative urge (*Schmucktrieb*), and the mimetic urge (*Nachahmungstrieb*), seen as progressively more sophisticated manifestations of the one central tendency; together with speculations on the schizophrenic fascination with a personal symbolism and the tendency towards symmetry or at least rhythmical form—the last being a semi-veiled excursion into aesthetics. After this survey of general characteristics comes a lengthy section, not the least interesting, devoted to the presentation of ten individual cases of considerable power (a number of which are considered in the present book). Here Prinzhorn follows Morgenthaler's lead in naming the patients, giving them so to speak full status as artists; though he seems less involved than Morgenthaler in the private worlds he is describing—possibly because he had only met about half of the ten, none of whom were his 'own' patients.**

Here one may detect an ambivalence in Prinzhorn's stance. Whereas the notation of particular data is effected in a cool, scientific manner, the generalizations he draws lead him away into an area where he finds it difficult to resist a more 'metaphysical' tinge to his vocabulary. The

---

* In a discussion at the symposium on surrealism at Cerisy in 1966, the psychiatrist Gaston Ferdière asserted that for him true insanity meant schizophrenia, all other mental disorders being comparatively shallow.

** My own searches in the Heidelberg collection, which still remains inaccessible to the general public, led to the discovery of a whole sheaf of extraordinary coloured drawings by Joseph Sell. In his study of this artist, Prinzhorn seems to have ignored these, the impression given by the drawings he reproduces being much too bleak. I would hope that these pictures can be published at some future date, since circumstances prevented my featuring Sell adequately in the present work.

psychiatrist defers to the art lover when Prinzhorn maintains 'Whoever is unable to experience a picture through perception without being overcome by an intellectual compulsion to explain and shed light, may be a good psychologist, but will necessarily bypass the essence of the created work.' Oddly enough, Prinzhorn talks about particular drawings without much evidence of emotion; it is in his general speculations that he becomes mystical. The contradiction stands, though, only if one insists that Prinzhorn ought to have been a clinical observer.

What then are Prinzhorn's conclusions? After all the time he spent looking at an extraordinary variety of material he seems unable to offer more than a few tentative conclusions as to the characteristic features of schizophrenic art. Unwilling to list formal schemata, he writes convincingly about his general impression of 'pointenlose Konsequenz'—the pointless or gratuitous consistency that seems to determine such art: the particular nuance of irresponsibility in fantasy, though noticeable in say Bosch or Kubin, is, says Prinzhorn, particularly frequent in schizophrenic art, where it gives rise to a *Fremdheitsgefühl*, a feeling of strangeness, of eerie rhythms that establish the work as irreducibly foreign to our sensibility. The reaction is obviously due to the fact that one is looking in on an autistic world that, by its very nature, turns away from normal reality. Prinzhorn speaks of the solipsism of typical works, which, though frightening to a certain extent, is the keynote of a rich, self-defining realm wherein the creative process goes on with the unreflecting spontaneity of natural growth. What this means is that Prinzhorn holds the *Kernvorgang* of artistic creativity to be most evident where cultural pressures are the most effectively evaded, as they are in madness—an assertion consistent with my central theme.

Though stressing what must be seen as the autonomy of each separate schizophrenic world, Prinzhorn veers away from the theme of cultural isolation in order to postulate the existence of general shared characteristics at the pre-rational level of creation. The comparative material on which he draws—carvings from the Congo which *are* strikingly similar to the work of Karl Brendel, medieval woodcuts which *do* show deformations of the human body like those adopted by some schizophrenics—points to the existence in man of an elementary artistic process that will necessarily emerge in similar form in the work of 'primitive' creators, be they lunatic, uncivilized or otherwise. Prinzhorn seems fairly confident that he has proven the existence of 'psychic forms of expression and their related visual formulations such as are of necessity almost the same in all men, given the same conditions, in the same way as physiological processes', a theory very close to Jung's notion of collective archetypes. Having said all this, Prinzhorn ends on a note of caution, stating somewhat curiously that only a biologically established norm can provide the basis for a proper critique of the comparative field.

Despite some contradictions, or rather hesitancies, Prinzhorn's still remains a remarkably stimulating book. In his closing remarks he says that the *Kernvorgang* in which the unconscious components of *Gestaltung* are embodied 'can be studied in no better material than this', and maintains that henceforth the demarcation line between the art of the insane and 'cultural' art can only be defended by a prejudiced conservatism. Though he does not explicitly state that madmen produce great art, the book essentially conveys a feeling of respect for works which he was the first to make known to anything like a wide public. If only for the wealth of illustrations, one can see why the surrealist painter Hans Bellmer might consider this book to be one of the major intellectual events of the century.

Since Prinzhorn's time psychiatric interest in the art of the insane has grown. Important books have been published by such authorities as Robert Volmat, Ernst Kris, Helmut Rennert and J. H. Plokker. The Société internationale de psychopathologie de l'expression held its seventh colloquium in Germany in September 1971, at which over thirty papers were read. The climate of opinion is such that an eminent psychiatrist like Dr Alfred Bader of Lausanne now feels in a position to state quite calmly that 'there is properly speaking no such thing as psychopathological art, for the artistic phenomenon, the creative act are not modified in their essence by mental illness', and to proceed to discuss the drawings of his patients in terms of their originality as works of art.

A dominant figure at present is Dr Leo Navratil of Vienna, whose book *Schizophrenie und Kunst* (1965) is an admirably succinct guide to the field. Navratil's definition of schizophrenia takes into account the development of research from the time Eugen Bleuler replaced Kraepelin's term *dementia praecox* with that of schizophrenia, denoting not one illness but a group of related psychic disorders. Broadly speaking, these are characterized by a faulty co-ordination of the affective, the intellectual and the motor functions (Stransky), having the effect of dissociating the normal regulating mechanism of reasoning from the henceforth vulnerable emotional self. Though catatonic insensitivity can be a symptom of schizophrenia, this does not imply a loss in affective amplitude in the schizophrenic, which can often be abnormally high (Bleuler, Mette). In the acute phase of schizophrenia there is a total collapse of the original structure of the self, accompanied by a panic sense of loss. But as the exaggerated affects decrease in intensity, there begin to emerge new patterns of behaviour whose function is to rehabilitate the personality—though the model is other than that of the sane personality. This structuring process, though in effect it confirms the psychotic alienation of the schizophrenic, and hence deserves to be called 'illness', might in fact equally well be called an attempt at cure (Freud). One of the symptoms of schizophrenia is artistic expression, usually in the form of writing or drawing, and Navratil attributes to such activity a re-formative function, whereby the elaboration of artistic forms engineers the stabilization of the personality and, in some cases, the beginnings of some contact with the surrounding world. Navratil can thus state: 'The creative achievement of these patients is a symptom of illness, and the formative process at its base is a process governed by that illness, more precisely, an attempted reparation (*Restitutionsversuch*) within the sphere in which the illness takes place.'

When the schizophrenic projects his inner fantasy-world, he does so at such a pitch of intensity that to him the ordinary world appears doubtful, null, derealized. Yet the world into which he retreats does not necessarily enclose a luxuriant jungle: the mechanisms of restitution tend to create an ordered self. This helps to explain the impression of *deliberateness* that many schizophrenic drawings convey. If there *is* intentionality about the activity, it seems only logical that Navratil should follow the example of Rennert, who in *Die Merkmale schizophrener Malerei* (1962) had catalogued the stylistic traits of schizophrenic art in a way that Prinzhorn, for example, had been loath to do. That such lists do not serve any diagnostic purpose has become abundantly clear, for the traits mentioned—intensification of contours, mixed profile, geometricization, condensation of pictorial elements, trans-parency effect—may be pointed out in the works of countless perfectly sane artists, especially of the post-cubist era. Navratil's intentions are descriptive rather than diagnostic. Lately he has offered four main tendencies as guidelines: formalization; deformation; use of symbols; and physiogno-micization (the tendency to impose facial interpretation on shapes); and speaks of the schizophrenic 'style' as being 'unreal, anti-naturalistic, dis-integrated, mannerist, original'. Drawing an analogy with the mannerist trend in European art as defined by G. R. Hocke (*Die Welt als Labyrinth*, 1957), a formal one based on shared stylistic habits, Navratil speaks of schizophrenic art as being the true 'primitive gesture of mannerism', an anti-classical art that is not derivative of any tradition. The sense here is that schizophrenic art is an authentically original, i.e. non-conformist art.

Navratil holds to Prinzhorn's intuition that a single psychic process is operative in the art of sane as of insane artists, so that there is no need to speak of 'schizophrenic creativity' but of creativity pure and simple. All art is of a piece in that its aim is self-realization. 'Creativity is neither a privilege of the mad nor yet of the genius, but an everyday phenomenon.'

The suggestion is based on the clear impossibility of differentiating between individual beings on the crude basis offered by the polar terms 'sick' and 'healthy'. It is with this in view that Navratil organizes public exhibitions of engravings prepared by the inmates in his Austrian clinic, to promote some sort of contact between what goes on inside and outside its walls. One might be tempted to ask how far Navratil can go and still remain a practising psychiatrist. In a recent text he quotes with evident approval the romantic poet Novalis, who conjectured that man might discover all kinds of new possibilities if he were to begin to love sickness; and cites two Viennese artists: Ernst Fuchs, who sees madness as the logical next step after reason in the dialectic leading to true intellectuality; and Arnulf Rainer, who calls madness 'the thirteenth muse'.

Rainer has developed the notion of the creative richness of schizophrenia to the point where he is able to maintain that it has been at the root of all that has been most original in art since the days of Romanticism, and is likely to be as important a factor in future art as was the Negro model at the turn of the century. Rainer's enthusiasm extends beyond relatively 'safe' works such as drawings to embrace other modes of expression far less likely to find public acceptance—gestures, grimaces, catatonic seizures, and comparable 'happenings', even primitive physiological functions. All form part of what he terms 'catatonic art' (*Katatonenkunst*), an art which, he suggests, has its origins in the grimacings and gesturings of man's earliest evolutionary stage. The self-engrossed manifestations of madness constitute an unique medium, an 'autistic theatre' (*autistisches Theater*) wherein creator, work and audience are identical.

The artistic propensities of the mad are for Rainer evidence enough that, far from being relegated to a side-show, their productions should be recognized as an autonomous culture in its own right. The *Irrenkultur* (culture of the insane) is at present undergoing persecution at the hands of the medical profession, which, in censoring most of its manifestations, is attempting a species of euthanasia. There are still only two or three proper collections of insane art—more should be started. Hospitals should no longer be permitted to burn the drawings of those artists of talent that, on a purely statistical calculation, must exist, yet who never reach an audience, thanks to the prejudiced attitude of psychiatrists like the one Rainer quotes as saying that schizophrenic artists entertain 'a generally false certainty of the excellence of what they do'. Rainer goes on to exclaim that the mad should be allowed to set up their own Institute for Insane Culture—or at least, he argues, we the sane should make reparation for Hitler's mass-murder of mental patients by establishing a museum to their memory, to contain works and documents by the mad. For the time being Rainer organizes regular public showings of his own considerable collection of mainly Eastern-European material.

Several hypotheses are now possible. Perhaps, as Rainer seems to think, schizophrenia is not a malady, but simply a peculiarly acute form of discourse with the self, a creative activity that we all practise daily, albeit with less intensity. Perhaps *all* art is 'pathological' to the extent that it involves a dissociation of the subjectivity from commonplace surroundings and manifests itself in bouts of engrossed self-expression. All art proceeds from the same central urge, says Prinzhorn. We must abandon terms like 'sick' and 'healthy', says Navratil, schizophrenia being only an extreme of the continuum of human psychological experience.

In his history of insanity in the Age of Reason, *Histoire de la folie* (1961), Michel Foucault designates the 'gesture that divides madness (from reason)' as constituting itself a form of madness, implying that this 'act of scission' cuts across the essential unity of man, even though it may preserve the society we live in. The metaphor of a 'sick society', manifesting its sickness above all in its insistence on the outrageous norm of health, is one of tested relevance, whether it be used to describe the society that condemned Expressionist art as *entartete Kunst* (degenerate art), or the capitalist conformities of today. At present, says Foucault, there is no common language between the 'sane' and the 'mad'. Exchange has broken down, and 'the language of psychiatry, which is a monologue of reason *about* madness, has been established only on the basis of such a silence'. What can be done, now? The psychiatrist R. D. Laing's recommendation is that notice must be taken of the unconscious strategic moves that people make when they are together. These form a basis for society, and they must be rendered conscious for all. A proper syntax of communication must be established if autistic theatre is to come across to a wider public than the isolated self. The peripheral yet fecund activities of *Irrenkultur* may constitute an alarming threat to the culture of *society as we know it*, but it may also be that man must confront its challenge if he is to preserve any sense of justice and wholeness.

Dubuffet and art brut

One of the most adamant champions of the art of the alienated is Jean Dubuffet, an ardent collector of what he calls 'art brut'. The concept embraces not only the art of the clinically insane, but also other art of an authentically untutored, original and extra-cultural nature. He began collecting material of this kind early in 1945, when he undertook methodical searches in Switzerland. After collecting assiduously for three years, he was able in 1947 to open a small 'institute' in Paris, the Foyer de l'Art Brut. Small exhibits of items from the collection attracted enough interest for Dubuffet to found in 1948 the Compagnie de l'Art Brut, in conjunction with André Breton, Jean Paulhan, Charles Ratton, H.-P. Roché and Michel Tapié. In new premises, the company put on exhibitions of drawings by Wölfli, Aloïse, Heinrich Anton M., Jeanne Tripier and others. Soon enough material had been collected for a large-scale public exhibition of two hundred items at the Galerie Drouin in 1949. The catalogue contained Dubuffet's peremptory manifesto 'L'Art brut préféré aux arts culturels'. A few years later, however, the company had to be dissolved for lack of capital and space, and, taking full charge of the collection, Dubuffet decided to ship it to the United States, placing it in the safekeeping of the painter Alfonso Ossorio. There it remained for ten years, until it was recovered in 1962, at which time the Compagnie de l'Art Brut was re-instituted, with Dubuffet as president. More material had been found for the collection, which now numbered over a thousand items—drawings, paintings, carvings, embroideries, etc.—by a hundred artists, of whom about fifty were considered to be of major importance. At this time the company took over premises in the rue de Sèvres—a four-storied building that houses the whole collection, a library and photographic documents. A series of richly illustrated publications under the title *L'Art Brut* began to appear in 1964, comprising studies of all the main artists of interest, largely written by Dubuffet himself. By 1966, eight issues had come out, covering about fifty cases. An important exhibition of art brut was mounted at the Musée des Arts décoratifs in 1967, and in 1971 a bulky catalogue listing over four thousand items was published. In September 1971 the Compagnie de l'Art Brut was dissolved and an agreement signed with the City of Lausanne whereby the collection will eventually be transported to that city for permanent display in the Château de Beaulieu.

The catalogue of the 1967 exhibition was prefaced by Dubuffet's text 'Place à l'incivisme' ('Make way for barbarism'), in which he explains his standpoint as follows: 'The aim of our enterprise is to seek out works that as far as possible escape cultural conditioning and proceed from truly original mental attitudes.' One does not expect of art, he says, that it should be *normal*: it must be original and unpredictable, otherwise it will not affect

Adolf Wölfli *Saint-Adolf-Grand-Grand-God-Father* 1915
Prinzhorn collection, Heidelberg

us. Only art that embodies an authentic *pureté brute* (raw purity) can be expected to convey anything like a true dynamism. All other kinds of art are so to speak *cooked*—according to the fastidious recipes drawn up by the chefs of culture.

Dubuffet believes that in modern society culture has come to mean indoctrination of the many by those few who, by mobilizing a considerable number of intellectual weapons (ideas like patriotism, civic pride, respect for the past, etc.) preserve an odious *status quo* of totalitarian proportions. Culture, he says, has become addicted to classifying and situating all products offered to it.*

Culture selects, filters, reduces, sterilizes. 'Simplifying, unifying, making uniform, the cultural machine, based on the elimination of flaws and scrap, on the principle of sifting in order to retain only the purest essence from its raw material, finally manages to sterilize all germination. For it is precisely from flaws and scrap that thought derives sustenance and renewal. A fixative of thought, the cultural machine has got lead in its wings.' One instance given in the specific field of art is the reliance on the word 'beauty', guaranteed to strike fear in the masses. In our culture, beauty is defined with respect to a norm whose 'objective' necessity is justified by hypocrisy and convention. But 'beauty is a pure secretion of culture as gall-stones are of the liver.' Equally sinister is the notion of *value*, attributed to works on an officially agreed scale. By setting an aesthetic value on mental products, and encouraging thoughtless assimilation of this with market value, the cultural machine—which has a virtual monopoly over valuation and the distribution of grades—maintains a demoralizing system in which people scarcely dare question the validity of what are, at bottom, mere cultivated illusions. The flourishing of cultural labels has the effect of blinding the public to the actual products on show, to a point where, Dubuffet says, *art culturel* has become the opium of the people. Worse still, culture deadens the creative instinct in people, for if they have culture thrust at them all the time they will feel hampered when it comes to expressing themselves naturally: they reach the point where they feel that to create art is necessarily to 'put on a performance' along set lines. Art informed by individual caprice appears illegitimate, and so those unskilled in the techniques nurtured by academicism, that is to say the greater mass of people, feel that art is something that can only be produced by the trained professional—any untutored activity being suspect or 'mad'.

According to Dubuffet, the basic confusion springs from the word *culture*

* The present publication, as perhaps any book on art brut, is bound to submit to the charge of being part of the same process.

itself. It has two meanings: (1) knowledge of and deference to works from the past (or at least those works whose survival has been engineered by the historians of Art); (2) the active development of individual thinking. What has happened is that the first meaning has come to asphyxiate the second. This dictatorship of the past over the present is something that Dubuffet cannot stomach. He even rages over the necessity to use an inherited language, French, to express himself, and when he writes, he does so in a style clearly intended to cut out the stylistic graces that are the pride of the cultivated Frenchman. He has even experimented in verbal distortions and vulgar slang in an effort to restore to language something of the primordial savagery that has been silenced by *le beau parler*. Dubuffet recognizes of course that it is impossible to de-condition oneself completely, but at least one should strive for more independence from the imposed norm. Possibly, he says, the only real solution would be an institute of de-culturalization run by especially lucid teachers who, over a period of years, would create a current of triumphant negativism, and by awakening 'la vivifiante faculté d'OUBLI' (the invigorating faculty of FORGETFULNESS) achieve a scouring-out of the whole machinery of the mind, leaving it in gleaming order for *new* thoughts.

Meanwhile Dubuffet sets his sights on particular attitudes of mind approximating to this ideal solution. His principle is mobility, his thought typified by a kind of vigorous caprice. He wants to avoid the immobilizing effect of *idées fixes*, and turns towards what is agile, exciting, and fecund. His preference always goes to things that are unformed and chaotic, things that have an irrational vitality. His taste is neatly exemplified when he contrasts the placid, humanist, morally stable art of the Graeco-Roman tradition with the burlesque, barbarian, pan-vitalist current which he calls 'Nordic'. Above all he loves proliferation. In a marvellous evocation of the Paris flea-market, he describes with great excitement the thronging crowds and the stands on which are 'exhibited' hundreds of wristwatches or potato-peelers or padlocks, and declares that 'it is swarming chaos which enriches and enlarges the world, restoring it to its true dimensions and its true nature.' Horizontal proliferation is what is healthy, whereas the vertical structure of culture—the hierarchical pyramid of official values— is unhealthy. Against the anaemia of what are known as 'the fine arts'— the very expression suggests delicate sickliness—Dubuffet proposes the regenerative cacophony of art as it spurts forth from 'the viscera and the solar plexus'. This is true *création d'art* (artistic creativity).

It is not to be understood that Dubuffet is advocating sheer amputation of sensitivity such as would reduce men to vegetables. The attitude he is defending is in fact one of extreme mental alertness, for 'in truth the fecund attitude is that of refusing and disputing culture, rather than that of merely

Aloïse *Panier fleuri ô colombe (quo vadis)* (*Basket with flowers oh dove (quo vadis)*) between 1948 and 1950 Collection de l'Art Brut, Paris, courtesy Jean Dubuffet

August Neter *Landscape* Prinzhorn collection, Heidelberg

being uncultured. . . . The important thing is to be *against*.' For Dubuffet is above all an intelligent *individual*, and he prizes *la regimbe*, the insubordinate attitude, which he cultivated during his army 'career' and tries to maintain in his 'career' as an artist. 'Systematic refusal, obstinacy, the spirit of contradiction and paradox, the attitude of unsubmissiveness and revolt'— these are the qualities that he instinctively asks of original creation. Let it not be supposed that this implies a studied deviation from the norm such as in turn creates a cultural stereotype, as did the wilful eccentricity of certain aesthetes in the Paris of 1900. Dubuffet would have his individualist indifferent to fashion, indeed indifferent to any audience. When he dedeclares that 'the production of art can only be conceived as individual, personal and done by all (*faite par tous*)', he manages to combine the virtues of the distinct individual with those of the anonymous, proliferating masses. Though paradoxical, the notion of this 'anonymous separatist' is a forceful one.

Dubuffet's ideal individualist would not be Van Gogh, the Douanier Rousseau, or one of the surrealist painters; for, he says, all these artists did was to produce works whose relation to authentic art brut is like that of going on a luxury cruise in the Pacific to being shipwrecked on a desert island. That is, a more integral posture of dissociation from the cultural system is required before one can speak of genuine art brut. Only what grows naturally and is projected spontaneously from within the psychic depths of the artist can be considered valid as original form: all else remains tainted or distorted by *idées reçues*.

The strongest applicants for recognition under these rigorous conditions are bound to be the insane, since madness is *par excellence* the refusal to conform, and the cultivation of individualism. In Dubuffet's view, people overstress the loss side in madness: why not consider the profits? For him, madness is not a negative but a positive, its contribution to human life not unhealthy but regenerative.

Other types of people may also qualify as producers of art brut. Here the same conditions must be fulfilled, though the problems of gauging whether there has been, for instance, any exposure to *art culturel* are perhaps greater. In the case of those who purport to create works of art while in a mediumistic trance, the evidence will sometimes point to a genuine case of spontaneous creativity; often it will be possible to draw a valid analogy with the self-contained mechanisms operative in schizophrenia, to the extent, that is, that the medium tolerates a minimum of interference from others during the creative process. As for the postulate of a spirit-realm with which mediumistic artists might claim to be in communication, this is something that Dubuffet commonsensically resists, holding that the creative process is the fruit of 'a continuum of the mind' such that all true 'inspirations' are on a par. It is very likely, he says, that the explanation of intervention on the part of spirit voices or supernatural forces amounts to an alibi invented as a defence against ridicule. If other people do not recognize the activity of artistic creation as legitimate, personal 'inspiration' may escape this social stricture if its products can be attributed to a more distant agency. For Dubuffet, though, the work of a Madge Gill is by her own hand rather than that of her 'spirit guide' Myrninerest.

The other types of people whose work is relevant to Dubuffet's enquiry may be loosely referred to as the 'innocent' (I shall speak later of the implications of the word 'naïf', which I am avoiding). These are by and large people who for various reasons have managed to elude the full warping effects of culture, and who, despite superficial signs of indebtedness to, for example, folk art (as in the case of Bogosav Živković) or more idiosyncratic hobby-horses (as with Joseph Moindre's passion for egyptology), manage nonetheless to achieve a distinctly individual style. Often it appears that the psychic pressures of a truly personal vision determine the social life of such an artist. Many of the artists in Dubuffet's collection, if not as literally isolated as the hermit Clarence Schmidt, live to some extent *en marge*, at a remove from their surroundings.

Where one uses the phrase 'minimum conditioning' one is close to saying 'lack of education'. There is indeed a fairly high incidence in Dubuffet's collection of artists who had little or no schooling. In strict terms of 'culture' this betokens a limited knowledge, but bears no necessary relation to intelligence, nor to creative proficiency. Dubuffet considers it yet another flagrant example of cultural prejudice that people suppose only educated people can create good art. He points to the example of the medium Augustin Lesage, who left school at fourteen to work in the mines. Lesage's first paintings, which he began to produce some twenty-one years later, are marvels of intricate design. The later paintings deteriorated, according to Dubuffet, as Lesage began to pick up some elements of education. It is, he goes on, a characteristically French prejudice to suppose that an uneducated man is strictly incapable of producing a convincing drawing. In countries like Spain, Italy and Yugoslavia, nobody finds it odd for a peasant to devote himself to painting or poetry. As with madness, there is a factor of compensation, it seems: deficiency in one area can be accompanied by a corresponding abundance in another. Certain analphabets he has met, states Dubuffet, have struck him as being of highly developed intellect.

This belief in the mental strength of the artists he most admires leads Dubuffet to argue that *they know perfectly well what they are doing*. The phenomenon of inspiration is thus not to be explained as submission to unconscious dictation, in a way reminiscent of surrealist automatism. In the first place, Dubuffet will even contest that madness is necessarily something that 'imposes' itself. Consistent with his positive evaluation of the condition is his theory that many psychotics deliberately 'choose' madness as a means of escaping from an arid social life. The *aliéné*—the common French term for madman is illuminating here—is someone who chooses to step aside from conformity and set up an alternative system of ideas and behaviour conducive

Heinrich Anton M. *Two faces* 1917–22
Collection de l'Art Brut, Paris, courtesy Jean Dubuffet

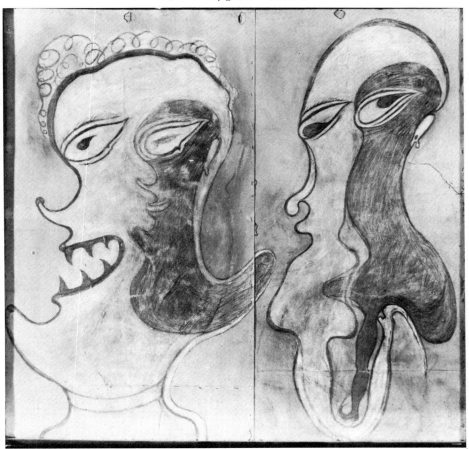

to fuller satisfaction of his psychic needs. Thus the schizophrenic Heinrich Anton Müller was, says Dubuffet, in love with his alienated condition. He was able to re-invent his life along the lines most appealing to himself, and was therefore always able to remain jubilant. 'It is jubilation that the *aliéné* is seeking. All that impairs this derives, in his eyes, from erroneous visions which must be reformed.' Perhaps sanity is the madness that the schizophrenic refuses; he is right to do so if by creating his own self-engrossed art he can derive deep delight from the spectacle. Rainer's idea of 'autistic theatre' would seem to be perfectly apposite.

Dubuffet is at pains to qualify what might seem like an impossibly extremist viewpoint when he states that in applying the notion of art brut to the facts of artistic production one is in truth appealing to an 'ideal pole', a limit-point which no artist could be expected actually to reach. 'Art brut, savagery, freedom, these should not be conceived as places, nor above all as fixed places, but as directions, aspirations, tendencies.' After all, an adult person, whatever his mental or social condition, cannot be supposed to have escaped all external influences! The unlikely case might be the autistic child who absolutely resists treatment until adulthood; but such a person would be highly unlikely to be artistic—though, to follow Rainer's line of thinking, there is no telling what fantasy spectacle might not go on within the autistic mind.

This extreme hypothesis points to a problem which I shall take up again later: the logical conjunction of progressive alienation and progressive breakdown of communication. At the 'ideal pole' we share nothing with the artist, and he cannot offer us anything, even if he wished to, for we lack the basis of any dialogue with his work.

But is communication always a *sine qua non*? Dubuffet seems inclined to accept the total validity of the 'imaginary public' which the self-absorbed artist invents for himself. This audience, he suggests, is perfectly adequate. 'It is not just because a work has been destined by its author for his own exclusive use that we should deny it the character of *création d'art*.' Indeed Dubuffet comes close to saying that the artist is all the more admirable if he hides his work from others—schizophrenics can be very secretive and possessive about their work—and he suggests that this might in fact make the work more interesting to us when it does come to light. Rather than worry about the impossible extreme case, Dubuffet overcomes the contradiction between autism and communication by supposing that the private rituals of art are productive of psychic intensities that do have an undeniable effect on others—be it only, at first, to create the *Fremdheitsgefühl* of which Prinzhorn spoke.

In *Asphyxiante culture*, Jean Dubuffet deals with the situation of the anti-cultural artist faced with a system that demands conformity. This he must resist by turning completely away into an a-social posture, which informs the primary stage of activity, certainly the most significant, the totally absorbing process of creation and self-expression. The second stage is best described as anti-social, the making public of what has been created so as to make manifest that initial turning-away which constitutes the subversive meaning of his work. The position seems untenable: either the artist turns away completely and for good, or else in only half-turning his back he risks compromising his art. That is, he risks the deformation implicit, in Dubuffet's opinion, in the notion that one is creating with an audience in view: such art work easily slides into self-advertisement and loses its 'autistic' dynamism. The solution must lie, argues Dubuffet, with a sharp eye for nuance, in a mode of publication that stops short of publicity, a manner of communicating that does not utilize the insidious machinery of culture in order to reach an audience. In theory the two attitudes seem in exact contradiction, and elsewhere Dubuffet in fact categorically opposes the a-social/anti-social position with the social one, citing the 'exemplary' career of Simone Marye, who won praise as a talented young sculptress in the twenties from such writers as Alexis Léger and André Gide, but who, after having been hospitalized with Alzheimer's disease many years later, began to produce genuinely 'autistic' drawings while in a state of almost total withdrawal from reality (Dubuffet suggests maliciously that these would have shown up Gide's self-styled a-social pose as a sham if he had been confronted with them). But the extremes of a-social and anti-social activity—on the one hand, a lack of contact with society, on the other a sporadic, subversive contact—can be reconciled, and for this I would advance an example that I think fits Dubuffet's solution of publication-without-publicity. I am thinking of 'public relations' as conceived by the artist Scottie Wilson, who has exhibited his drawings in an empty shop on the Marine Parade, Margate —'Entry 6d'—and who jokes about selling them off in the streets 'like kippers, two at a time'. This artist's disdain for the blandishments of art galleries and the rest of the cultural system is quite exemplary.

As ever it is the presupposition that one is going to produce 'art' for others to look at that makes for a false situation and a cramping of the primary expressive urge. Such antagonisms will remain with us, says Dubuffet, until such time as art, ceasing to be projected by the mind outside itself as a label applicable to an external object (the picture on the wall), 'is integrated in such a form that thought, instead of facing it, is inside it'. Only when art ceases to be a 'thing' bearing a label will we be able to dispense with problematic terms like 'art' or 'culture' and, if I understand Dubuffet rightly, enter upon a new mode of creative receptivity. About this Dubuffet can, understandably, articulate little more than a lyrical prophecy.

For the moment, Dubuffet's counsel to those who are confronted with art brut is to reject that colossal prejudice of *le beau*—beauty which 'comes down to us directly from the song of angels and the burning bush' just so that learned professors of Aesthetics can point out its dogmas with cane in hand ... 'Beauty? Beauty my eye'. Dubuffet's 'aesthetics' are strictly *other*. The vocabulary he would use to evoke the impression received from true *création d'art* is of a different, more vital order. Terms such as *intéressant* or *passionnant* are indeed lacking in objective verification, unlike *beau*, which can be checked against an aesthetic canon. But Dubuffet, individual to the core, insists that objectivity smacks of 'value', and opts for personal caprice as the only real standard if one is to get any pleasure or instruction from art. 'I deny that there are beautiful colours and ugly colours, beautiful shapes and others that are not. I am convinced that any object, any place without distinction can become a key of enchantment for the mind according to the way one looks at it and the associations of ideas to which one links it.' At this new level any evaluation of the work of art must take account not of its plastic 'beauty' but of its greater or lesser capacity to stimulate the mind.

Authenticity and originality

I have defined the range of material designated as art brut as deriving from three broad types of artist—schizophrenics, mediums and innocents—though I have implied that these are not to be construed as distinct groupings linked to a system of classification, these three types being simply different manifestations of the one 'type' that I am defining. It may be useful, so that no confusion should arise, to give a fairly exhaustive listing of the kinds of art that I am *not* concerned with, with some hints as to the reasons why they are excluded from this book.

European folk arts such as the nineteenth-century *Heimatkunst* of the Appenzell region in Switzerland, or the peasant art of Sicily, may appear remote from the culture with which we are most familiar, but they are no less subservient to traditions both aesthetic and social. The anonymity of folk art only serves to underline the subordination of individual inventiveness to a cultural standard. Popular arts of various kinds—I am thinking of such things as the designs on playing cards or figureheads on ships—tend equally to a cultural stereotype that rarely shows significant variation. In these instances, art is very much an acquired craft, and we would be foolish to spend time over it in a search for *pureté brute*.

A more individualistic species of art, apparently closer to the specifications I have drawn up, is the art produced by naïve painters (sometimes referred to as autodidacts, neo-primitives, Sunday painters, etc.). These are individuals of usually humble background who, having received no formal training in art, take up painting at first as a hobby, later perhaps as a full-time activity. The term 'naïve' often carries a pejorative overtone as though to mock at the pretensions of these people, who are, by and large, striving for recognition as 'artists'. Culturally speaking, they are in a false position. They lack training in the academic skills (even though most manage to pick up the principles of perspective), yet they attempt to become the colleagues of professionals. In their efforts to create works that will if not rival at least belong in the same category as the works of those who command high fees and paint in spacious studios, the naïves are in a very real sense creating to order. Even if only 'playing to an imaginary audience', they are acting a part that is not consistent with their innermost selves, and their art thus risks becoming counterfeit.

What I am saying is borne out by the way in which over recent decades the cultural machinery has reacted to this odd quirk of creativity, and has undertaken to assimilate it and give it cultural status. Though it gains only second-class prizes for its 'prettiness', rather than for its beauty, art naïf seems generally content with its little niche in art history, and one cannot really claim that it is subversive. It has a *social* function; it hankers for integration. And although it would be a distortion to suppose that it is all of a piece—the touching primitivism of Alfred Wallis is a far cry from the polished professionalism of André Bauchant, whilst the delirious flowers of Séraphine Louis, the women of Morris Hirshfield and the unicorns of Ivan Generalić stand out as imaginative creations of some distinction—it can be concluded that in the majority of cases lack of technical skill does not conceal a derivative, if not consciously imitative posture. It must be recognized, in spite of all this, that in a number of cases the two foremost French authorities on art naïf and art brut, Anatole Jakovsky and Jean Dubuffet respectively, manage to lay claim to the very same artists, the medium Joseph Crépin being a case in point. In the present connection it should suffice to note that Jakovsky's requirements are less than clearly defined.

Another area worth mentioning is the art of prisoners, which Hans Prinzhorn studied in his *Bildnerei der Gefangenen* (1926). There is no *a priori* reason why in this area there should not emerge some authentic examples of art brut, given the conditions that may be assumed to prevail: internment, enforced leisure, isolation, anti-social attitudes. Prinzhorn's book contains some interesting illustrations of graffiti and figures modelled in bread, but there is much that is naïve and desultory. An explanation might be that internment in prison does not underline and so to speak 'justify' the psychic distancing from the outer world of those that are shut up in mental institutions. One might guess that prison is experienced much more as physical impediment, producing not imaginative escapism but an art that reflects a desire to re-join the society outside, even if this means the 'alternative' society of criminals. Even this sub-culture has its stereotypes, as is demonstrated by Prinzhorn's examples of tattoo designs done by criminals. That a shared mode of life and a single collective desire— release or escape—may impede the expression of *individual* vision in prisoners, seems to be well demonstrated by the dozens of near-identical soldiers and ships that were carved in bone by French prisoners at Norman Cross, near Peterborough, during the Napoleonic wars.

At first sight, child art strikes one as another obvious area for consideration. Do not children have an innocent, unstructured vision of things that their drawings reflect with artless immediacy? Certainly they do enjoy the lack of training that I have argued as being a positive virtue. Yet there are reasons why their work, however appealing, does not count as art brut. Dubuffet observes that the child's psyche is not very rich, and is thus unequal to that of the adult—not altogether a very convincing argument if one considers that the 'richer' psyche of the adult is quite likely to be crammed with cultural produce. More to the point is that children do not create spontaneously once they realize the interest shown in their work by their parents or teachers. Beyond a certain age they create with an audience in view, and with a self-exhibiting tendency that equates to an attempt to become integrated in society—an attempt diametrically opposed to that of the adult artist who turns his back on culture. Lastly, children lack the concentration of the mature mind and cannot be expected to generate as much psychic energy as an adult. They scarcely know what they are doing, and in their best works tend to be closer to the passivity of psychic automatism than to the deliberateness of art brut.

Many other types of artist may appear relevant to our concern. There are a number of cases of trained artists who went mad, and whose work underwent significant change as a result. Of these the most important cases are those of the lesser-known painters Richard Dadd, Ernst Josephson, and Carl Fredrik Hill; of the schizophrenic painter of cats, Louis Wain;* of the psychotic sculptor F. X. Messerschmidt; and the well-known example of Van Gogh. Despite the interest of such cases, the formal training these artists received places them in a category of their own. Similarly one must exclude the visionary work of Blake and the mediumistic drawings of the playwright Victorien Sardou as proceeding out of skills or cultural moulds not conducive to that total *pureté brute* which is our concern. Again, surrealist painters, even those who went mad like Unica Zürn or were emotionally unbalanced like Arshile Gorky, cannot be accepted when there is evidence of artistic formation or attentiveness to public reaction. Like some of the other artists I mentioned as seekers after the primitive—Kirchner, Klee, Pollock—the surrealists have not always managed completely to cast off culture, and many have foundered on the sandbanks of self-conscious technique. In much modern experimental painting that addresses its innovations at a public and aims only at formal novelty, there is a tendency to a characterless uniformity that is at the absolute antipodes of art brut.

What if one turns to the antipodes of our modern Western civilization and considers the case of primitive art, in the sense of art created by peoples whose mental and social functions are so remote from our own? The problem is an interesting one.

In his book *Primitive Art* (1962), Paul S. Wingert distinguishes several more or less divergent usages of the word 'primitive' that go to show how suggestive yet how vague it can be. Wingert first points out the use of the term by the Darwinian evolutionists of the nineteenth century, who on

---

* I subscribe to the view expressed by Dr D. L. Davies that the weird sequence of 'schizophrenic' cats drawn by Wain and long thought to reflect the progressive collapse of his personality quite possibly represents a series of conscious exercises in wallpaper design based on Persian carpet patterns.

discovering the life patterns of the natives of the Pacific Ocean, Africa and North America, considered these to represent an earlier cultural phase through which European civilization had long since passed. The derogatory flavour of this usage encouraged its application by certain historians of art to work that is technologically crude or puerile in expression. Here it simply denotes a lack of quality in every respect. In fact, of course, as Wingert's book amply demonstrates, the art of such peoples as the Baoule of the Ivory Coast or the Haida Indians of British Columbia constitutes a highly developed expression of cultures which, though very different from other cultures, nonetheless have achieved maturity within their own context.

The word has also been used by art historians in other confusing ways to denote an early stage within the historical development of painting in various European countries, as in Flemish or French primitive painting; or to refer to the untutored art of the *naïfs*. Chronological earliness is implicit in the former but not in the latter usage. Wingert goes on to point out yet more alarming misuses of the word in connection with the 'high' cultures of the Incas and the Aztecs, the paleolithic and neolithic cultures of prehistoric times, folk art, child art, and the art of the mad—the effect is to erase the boundaries of these areas and to encourage the thought that they are very much of secondary interest. I think it likely that a careful study of the way words like 'primitive' have been used in recent times would reveal some of the persistent conflicts in society with regard to artistic and social non-conformity: 'primitive' is a word that contains both a positive and a negative charge, and is a weapon shared by both champions and enemies of culture. Needless to say, my own use of the word is entirely positive in spirit.

The values connoted by the term 'primitive art' in the sense of the tribal arts studied by Wingert are for Dubuffet singularly vitalist ones: instinct, passion, caprice, violence, delirium. What most attracts him is the feeling of a direct correspondence between a way of life that issues out of 'the continuity of all things' with an art that articulates this sense. In comparison, Western culture is a garment whose cut does not fit our true movements. Yet though it diverges drastically from the *art culturel* of the West, primitive art is not quite the same thing as art brut. The enigmatic, formalized statues of Easter Island, the complex patterned blankets of the Tlingit Indians, above all the highly sophisticated bronze work of Benin in Nigeria, these are evidence that primitive art is bound to strict traditions and professional skills. Wingert states unequivocally that 'primitive art is not a free, un-controlled, and untutored creation.' Inherent conservatism is indeed such that there are very few tribes in which individual inventiveness is encouraged at all. The Malagan art of New Ireland is one of the rare exceptions. Each clan in that part of the world felt it necessary to stage regular ceremonies to honour its ancestors. These revolved around the Malagan itself, a large wood-carving which clan prestige demanded should be ever more spectacular. The carvers to whom the task was entrusted were thus encouraged to invent something original each time. However, even here 'originality' was limited by convention, the 'new' designs being simply elaborations of traditional elements. One might want at least to turn to the aboriginal art of Arnhem Land in Northern Australia, as did Karel Kupka in his promisingly titled book *Un Art à l'état brut* (1962). Admittedly aboriginal paintings on bark are governed by a system of mental representations—totemic, mythical— which constitute what one must, however reluctantly, call a 'culture'. What is attractive, however, is the way the aborigine appears, according to Kupka, less concerned about art as *product*—he will abandon the finished piece of bark without bothering to preserve it—than as *process*.

As I have shown, the 'alternative' art to which the present book is addressed is to be sought not in cultures different from our own, since these do not break away from cultural norms and set figurations, but in true artistic heresies *within* the boundaries of our immediate system. 'Primitivism' here means a refusal of standards and a search for new expressive forms whereby the artist makes as if to go back to the beginning and slowly develop a personal 'culture' of his own. Non-alignment and imbalance are fundamental to this sort of enterprise. Lack of education may also be frequent, though this is not a mark of mental weakness. Lack of previous training is a crucial criterion, and yet this does not imply lack of self-acquired skill. Art brut does not seek approval. It has for instance nothing to do with art therapy as practised in mental hospitals, where doctors nowadays encourage patients to paint or draw—a move that hampers spontaneity and makes for an art that, like that of the child, is directed less at self-expression than at eliciting praise or approval. An attitude of integral alienation is necessary before a self-contained world can be born. A *tabula rasa* of existing forms, an *écart absolu*—Fourier's formula for the act of distantiating oneself totally from one's conditioning—these are the prerequisites of inventive freedom. It is indeed, in Dubuffet's view, more important to stress this act of choice than the inventive faculty itself: 'It is not the inventive faculty that is at all rare (we are persuaded that it is extremely common) but the daring to give it free rein.'

Once the conditions are found, the 'original creative urge', in Prinzhorn's phrase, leads to expression. Art emerges spontaneously, in a way that in some cases is comparable to the sudden giving way of a dam before the pressure of water. Among the artists in Dubuffet's collection are a good many who began to create only after the age of forty or fifty—some after sixty—as though psychic pressure had, on reaching a particular pitch, suddenly stimulated them into feverish activity. Prinzhorn points out that in many of the cases he studied, artistic creativity started with great suddenness, out of the blue; other observations suggest that schizophrenia may act as the stimulus itself (rather than its favourable condition); though this seems not very probable in view of the many schizophrenics who have no artistic leanings.

When the mediumistic artist Madge Gill speaks of 'authentic revelation coming through', she may be describing what some might call 'inspiration', a creative event in which are combined the primary process (the emergence of forms from the instinctual or 'subliminal' level) and the secondary process (the elaboration of those forms at a higher or 'conscious' level). It may be that there is a particularly 'pure' collaboration of emotion and intellect operating to express the total personality in unconstrained fashion. This at least in those cases where stylistic liberty is, or tends to be, absolute.

Navratil has noted the way in which schizophrenic artists who progress towards a cure follow a development leading from imaginative deformation to naturalistic representation of the most conventional and boring kind. Cure in this context suggests an abandonment of originality for the sake of colourless conformity. Whether or not psychiatrists feel regret about this is not an issue I need discuss; the observation serves principally to confirm the association of a non-conventional attitude in the artist with a refusal to copy *what is there* or to fabricate along impersonal lines. Between the poles of naturalistic art and total abstraction there are an infinite number of points, as both Prinzhorn and Dubuffet observe, and all artists of originality will offer forms that, when compared to actual reality; will appear as deformations. Truth to a personal vision means divergence from conventional vision; in any case, argues Dubuffet, the way in which people are conditioned to recognize a given form as 'true to life' is in fact arbitrary. A child's or a madman's scribble is sometimes offered as a representation of a very specific thing: the creator seems to have no difficulty in recognizing what for others is misshapen if not utterly formless. 'Derealization' does not mean lack of any reality at all, but an intensification of a distinct reality. The crude shapes carved on the walls of his wooden cell by the 'violent' patient Clément emerge in Dubuffet's meticulous study as the receptacles of a host of meanings. Here lack of precision in forming recognizable shapes is interpreted as the deliberate cultivation of multivalent allusion. The difficulty one has in 'reading' the embroidery of Elise lies in its highly elliptical style, not in any expressive deficiency. The most original works of art brut are effective to the extent that they sustain the tension between

Madge Gill Composition with faces
Newham (London) collection, courtesy James Green

the poles of representation and abstraction, particular statement and
generalization. The accent is here laid on the intensity of the creative act.
What Dubuffet refers to as *profondeur mentale*, mental depth, is gauged by
reference to the relationship between these poles. Here one might point to
the work of Madge Gill, which oscillates between figuration and pure
ornamentation in a way that creates a strong sense of vertigo. The effect
seems to be both instinctual and cerebral.

The problem for the autodidact is to find a personal language that
contains a minimum of borrowings. The notion of an involuntary art is
not very apposite in this connection. Dubuffet, for instance, insists on the
deliberateness with which the madman Heinrich Anton Müller forged his

41

artistic vocabulary of strange figures. The vigilant care he exercised in composing his drawings of monstrous faces suggests he was trying to develop the element of *strangeness* to the maximum. It is intriguing to consider that the *Fremdheitsgefühl* that Prinzhorn says is our principal reaction to schizophrenic works might indeed be the result of lucid intention! 'One is almost always mistaken', maintains Dubuffet, 'when one attributes to the authors of works which surprise us a lack of awareness of their strangeness.'

Nobody would deny the high pitch of concentration involved in the creation of art brut, and, as far as its most original representatives are concerned, a control of the chosen medium sufficient to dissuade anyone from associating it with inadequate skill. Alfred Bader refers to the 'intuitive certainty' shown in the best schizophrenic drawings as the hallmark of the true artist. But how 'original' can one force oneself to be? In inventing a personal language, each artist must, by the very reason of his distinctness, be creating a repertoire of patterns that, for all its variety, will be limited. No artist can fashion a non-derivative style again and again. Schizophrenic art has indeed been subjected to severe analysis by psychiatrists who come to somewhat deadening conclusions, as does Ernst Kris when he states that the 'modes of expression remain unchanged once the psychotic process has reached a certain intensity.' Or as Jean Vinchon would have it: 'Schizophrenic drawings are stereotyped.' Nobody would deny that 'iterations'— repetitions of formal elements such as hatching, circles, zigzags, dots, etc.— are pronounced features of much schizophrenic art. What one should be looking at, though, is the *use* to which the given limited formal repertoire is put. Wölfli's 'little birds', slugs and 'Hoptiquags' are shapes repeated again and again in his work. Yet their effect is not to create monotony but to sustain rhythms of great power. The autistic world may seem cramped from outside; within is a richness, an inventiveness such as art critics always like to tell us is most stimulated in conditions of constraint. Here the order is promoted by something instinctive, as Morgenthaler suggests, and—as Dubuffet says of Salingardes—refinement does not necessarily exclude invigorating qualities of nigh barbaric vitality. For all its repetitions, Wölfli's art is never dead.

At the end of his book on schizophrenia and art, Navratil comes to the conclusion that it is the personal note that makes for original art. This note arises where the artist is not a talented copyist of objective models, but a person who 'lets go' and, allowing aspects of his personality other than the social one to 'take over', arrives at an abnormal, non-aligned position. The creative process is conditioned by this collapse of ego-control. 'Primarily, artistic creativity is precisely not under the direction of the ego,

Adolf Wölfli *Riesen-Stadt, Waaben-Hall, mitsamt dem gleichnamigen, Skt.*
Adolf-Ring, ditto, Schatz'l-Ring (Giant town, Honeycomb Hall, along with one of the
same name, St Adolf Ring, ditto, Darling Ring) 1917
Kupferstichkabinett der öffentlichen Kunstsammlung, Basle

Augustin Lesage *Composition* (signed Léonard de Vinci)
Institut métapsychique international, Paris

but serves the purpose of *finding the ego* (*Ichfindung*)—and through the ego, of establishing a relation to the world—even if this aim is not always attained.' Whether or not the relation to the world is actualized, or whether or not we agree that schizophrenia does aspire to this end, the remark is generally illuminating. Whereas Plokker asserts that it is only *by chance* that psychotic artists find the 'significant form' that permits the adequate expression of their private reality, Dubuffet, taking over the paradox that some advanced psychiatrists have propagated, namely that madness is at once sickness and cure, might well argue that 'significant form' is available to anyone who 'lets go' fully. If, as Navratil thinks, all artistic creativity has the primary function of expressing the true nature of the interior self, and, building as it were from this central locus, can recreate the self as a genuine whole, then one can say that 'originality' will be the impression conveyed when the process is most complete. It was precisely thanks to the deliberate cultivation of a fantasy world that the schizophrenic artist Aloïse attained a lost balance, and reached a stage where, if not quite 'cured' in the clinical or social sense, as Jacqueline Porret-Forel recognizes at the close of her study *Aloïse et son théâtre*, she managed to construct a stable and lucid personality. Art can offer the sense of unity that society has removed, and is in this non-medical sense 'therapeutic'. Such a highly personal cure amounts to a critique of the reality from which the subject remains estranged.

The idea that art brut is often the result of a process of self-discovery is implicit in the argument that its dynamics arise from an exacerbation of individualism. Many of its works are self-portraits, or at least portrayals of the way the inner self sees itself. Scottie Wilson and Madge Gill, Wölfli and Aloïse, these all tend to project an idea of themselves into their art, and it is only natural that *self*-expression should take this form. Aloïse's pictorial universe is of course not only peopled with feminine presences; yet Mme Porret-Forel can argue that 'since Aloïse is herself a whole formed by all the elements composing the world as she has re-created it, she is her-self a universe, and each one of the pictures she draws represents herself, also.' Each spectacle in the autistic theatre constitutes a facet of the personality, and such art can truly be described, in Rainer's formula, as 'self-reproduction'. Dubuffet sees autistic art in just this way, as a process of fixing one's fluid fantasies so as to be in a position to contemplate them objectively, and thus enjoy the complicity of a 'pure dialogue with oneself'. This means jubilant cultivation of all that is most idiosyncratic to oneself and tends to be an exaltation, an 'intensification of what is individual' (Navratil) that leads to a truly *original* position. This insistence on one's unique identity as an artist does not imply a 'cure' in the sense of reintegration into society, which, as Rainer stresses, means a minimalization of

44

individuality. It is integration of the self on terms *other* than those of society that makes for the less 'acceptable' but more profound and vital art.

To talk of art brut is, then, to talk about a large number of independent artistic worlds that ought not to be envisaged as forming a block, much less a school. I think it crucial to insist on the notion of discrete, autonomous realities. This may be underlined by reference to some ideas of Von Uexküll, who in his *Theoretical Biology* is led to suppose not that each animal in a given area shares more or less the same 'environment', but that, given the different life style of each type of animal, each will possess a specific environment of its own. There are, he puts it, as many spaces and times as are contained in and determined by the individual's functional circle. He coins the expression 'island of senses' (*Sinnesinsel*) to characterize this. The line of thought could well be applied in the sphere of human psychology, in so far as each individual enjoys a separate consciousness of reality, i.e. a 'personal reality' determined by what might be called his own particular 'island of sensibility'. Schizophrenia is the extreme example of this—the shipwreck of the social personality on an island 'entire of itself'. It constitutes a self-contained kingdom in which what goes on is no longer reality-orientated thinking but magical thinking, or as Prinzhorn puts it: not a thinking, but a wishing.

The description I have given is of a hypothetical limit-condition such as I have indicated is more tendency than fact, even in the most acute cases. Navratil cites the psychiatrist H. Kranz as being satisfied that, over a large period of time, one can observe certain general changes in schizophrenic drawings that can only be attributed to the evolution of a society's history. In his view, schizophrenics *are* sensitive to what goes on in the outer world—wars, scientific discoveries, technological and artistic developments do leave an imprint of a particular time on their art. And Dr Maria Rave-Schwank points out that nowadays the religious obsessions that Prinzhorn found predominant in the period he was dealing with (the Heidelberg collection covers the years 1890–1920) are the exception rather than the rule. Schizophrenic art is thus subject to 'fashions'.

Yet I still feel that the notion of a pure autistic art as I have outlined it hitherto remains relevant as an ideal pole to orientate our thinking about art brut. This is especially necessary in the context of public reaction. Dubuffet has asked: 'Is it necessary—as most people do, if one looks closely—to expect artistic creations to be personal, unusual, innovatory *only to a limited degree*, and in such a way that once this degree is passed (one ought to establish at exactly what point this occurs) they are *excessively so*, and thereby cease to come under art, instead taking their place amongst the forbidden aberrations?' For the time being, the term 'autistic art' perfectly defines the 'aberrations' that inspire this reaction. Towards such as these, Cultural Man's response must indeed be a negative shrinking away. But are we totally incapable of examining without prejudice the products of minds other than our own? What is 'different' is also enriching, and where autistic attitudes mean an aggravation of individualism and the consequent concentration of creativity that I have described, they produce an effect of such 'high voltage' that it would be cowardice not to try to experience them. It may be possible to go a good deal further than we think into the autistic world; not to try at all is to admit our own cultural solipsism.

Emmanuel Drawing no. 23, 1963
Collection de l'Art Brut, Paris,
courtesy Jean Dubuffet

Scottie Wilson *Vase*
Brook Street Gallery, London

The temptation and the challenge

When people are faced with something utterly novel, they feel unsettled and instinctively seize upon whatever aspects of the new thing seem to resemble things already known to them. The phenomenon may be exemplified by the names given to exotic marine species as they were discovered. Descriptive labels such as 'cat-shark' or 'sea-horse' were coined on the basis of a reassuring analogy that could be drawn between those alien creatures of the ocean and the familiar creatures of the land. Though understandable, and to some extent unavoidable, such reactions are not always helpful: there is no useful comparison to be made between the behaviour of the sea-horse, for example, and that of an ordinary horse. The purely *formal* resemblance is of no help at all to the zoologist. Unproductive reactions of this kind can arise regarding the different species of art that have been mentioned above. When we are confronted with artistic productions which are so very different from what we know, the danger lies in falling back on the superficial similarities we think we can spot, and in imagining this is all the description we need to characterize the new. Those who, like Réja and Prinzhorn, ventured to point out a resemblance between the art of schizophrenics and the art of primitives or of children, involuntarily encouraged lazy generalizations about such art that have since become common currency. Thus one often finds people using a cliché of thought deriving from such comparisons, whereby 'the art of primitives-children-and-madmen' becomes a single category, a handy lumping-together that tends to make a diversity of material into a homogeneous mass without real variety, and hence without real value. Dubuffet has frequently pointed out the inadequacies of classifications based on superficial formal similarities and at best incomplete analogies between the thought-patterns of these groups of people.

Undoubtedly there is an element of imaginative stimulation in the suggestion that there is some kind of link between the farmyard and the ocean floor, between the nursery and the jungle, between, that is, the unknown and that which from being familiar may take on, all at once, an air of mystery. But this is cosy and unproductive fancifulness in comparison with the greater intellectual challenge laid down by the notion of *dissimilarity*.

Again, one can appreciate the intellectual attraction of Prinzhorn's premise, one that C. G. Jung was to expand upon a good deal, namely that the primary process operative in artistic work as far as possible untouched by the 'high' cultures, tends to produce recurrent motifs—the so-called archetypes—explained as being innate shapes imprinted on the collective psyche of all men, and equating to a shared physiological characteristic such as the habit of standing upright. One can feel excited at the

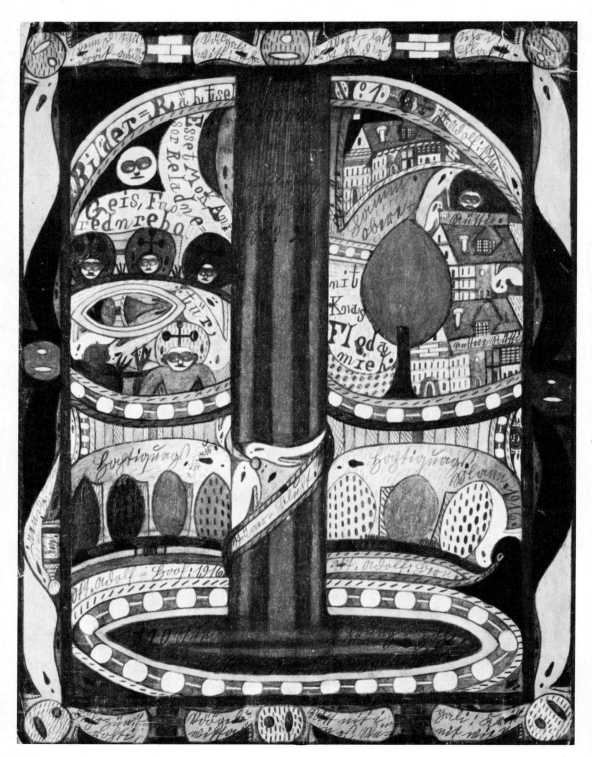

statement of the anthropologist Franz Boas, in his book *Primitive Art* (1927),
to the effect that 'the mental processes of man are the same everywhere,
regardless of race and culture'. And one can guess at something of the
complex sociological and philosophical evolution that made it possible
for Schilder to compare his patient's work with the art of his time—the
time of Kandinsky's theories—and for Volmat, more recently, to draw a
parallel between psychopathological art and all modern art. Whether or
not these suggestions are all scientifically defensible, they are provocative
and therefore important moments in the history of modern thinking in
these areas. Furthermore, misconceptions can be fascinating in that they
tell us about the mentality of those that hold them. The surrealists' favourite
analogy between their system of thinking and that of the savage might
very well fall down if subjected to a strict test—there is an element of
Rousseauesque idealization to be reckoned with—yet it has served to
clarify what they mean when they speak of a mode of 'mythical' or affective
reasoning as an alternative to unemotional conceptual thought.

I would however like to call a halt to inspirations of this kind, at least
where art brut is concerned. There are occasions when it is more productive to stress dissimilarities instead of resemblances. We know about
the latter: now let us face up to the former. Already Morgenthaler was
unenthusiastic about comparing Wölfli's work with the products of contemporary artists. He gives the example of a house in the process of being
demolished by competent workmen and a house ravaged by earthquake:
at a given moment the two ruins will look alike. Yet one would be foolish
if one concluded that there was, logically, a reliable analogy to be drawn
between the processes that made them ruins. (Basically, Morgenthaler is
contrasting the *deliberate* breakdown of formal representation in post-
cubist art with the *involuntary* breakdown of Wölfli's world-picture.) I
would feel that whatever validity there may be in the various theories
concerning expressive archetypes or shared thought-processes, it is more
useful as far as art brut is concerned to stress the distinctness, the independence of the individual artist. Just as 'primitive art' breaks down into
hundreds of separate and autonomous types of art, art brut splinters into as
many different categories as there are artists. For Dubuffet, *art culturel* is but
one species in the zoology of art—a pampered racehorse which he compares
highly unfavourably with the teeming diversity of all the other species
available for attention.

Taking the example of the drawings of a schizophrenic such as Audrey,
I would want to stress that her activity is as much deliberate as involuntary.
By this I mean that while there may well be archetypal forms emerging as
she draws—one imagines a Jungian catching his breath at every curve!—

there is equally a strictly idiosyncratic tendency to break away from norms and to create what one must call her own language. Picking up Kris' statement that 'whereas common elements relate to the id, we might say that the differences are determined by the ego', I would want to leave aside the problem of the universality of the id and pay more attention to the contribution of the ego, i.e. of that part of the personality that has been structured on individualist lines. On such a basis I am pressing not for a reductive view that would admit the lowest common denominator of art brut, but rather for a productive view that would greet with enthusiasm and without prejudice the idea of a *diversity* so pronounced that each artist emerges as a separate, unique case. The personal signature of each would then be seen as delineating the boundaries of an independent territory of great expressive richness. Art brut is a teeming archipelago rather than a continent crossed by disputed borders. The only connection between each 'island of sensibility' is that they are all distinct from the cultural mainland. And the only assumption of 'likeness' I would want to work from would be the common likeness in the works of a single artist. Even here it would be necessary to consider the total production of an artist before allowing oneself to make generalizations. The ideal of Dubuffet would be to have the complete works of each artist intact in his collection; and even then one might still suffer from lack of contact with their creator, who alone embodies the process that links the separate products.

One may well ask whether it is possible to use the word 'art' when confronted with such highly exceptional works. The art historian Georg Schmidt is highly reluctant to consider schizophrenic works as art 'in the strict sense of the term', by which he means art as achieved within a particular socio-cultural context. Ludwig Binswanger also refuses to call the drawings of the insane 'art' on the grounds that they lack any relation to artistic models and traditions: they are *not* art inasmuch as they are a-historical, purely personal products. For Binswanger, a man can still create 'art' if he consciously breaks with a tradition, but *not* if he knew nothing of that tradition in the first place. These dubious criteria are, I think, a good example of blatant cultural prejudice, based as they are on a tautological definition of art as art-as-defined-by-culture. If art has anything at all to do with original creativity, I would suggest that the word 'art' can be retained—if the defenders of cultural historicism object, they will only draw attention to their narrow-mindedness. Perhaps, though, one should use it sparingly, eventually to dispense with it and all the fabrications to which it gives rise. As Dubuffet sees it, 'as long as the word "art" is *not* pronounced, true creative invention can be exercised in complete innocence and full health'.

Indeed, what is the most needed is to insist on the healthiness and the seriousness of art that diverges from normality in the ways I have described. No longer is it acceptable that people should go along to Bedlam on a Sunday for a good laugh. No longer should it be acceptable that art brut be dismissed as inferior or irrelevant stuff. I have maintained the qualification 'autistic' in connection with the creative work of these artists of non-alignment. What impact can autistic art have, what import for others? That there can be a response on our part, provided we do not hide behind our cultural walls, is highly probable. For even when works are created for strictly personal consumption, the tensions sustained in this intimate process can still be highly stimulating to others. In presenting in this book over twenty cases of such artistic activity, I do not hope to 'explicate' but to provide a possibility of response. I imagine that a sense of beauty is less likely to result than a sense of shock; perhaps there may also emerge a feeling of intensity and personal involvement that will provide a healthy alternative to cool aesthetic appraisal.

What one should seek is not to analyse the product so much as to attune onself with the creative process; not to spot masterpieces but to respond to the vitality of the expressive act itself. Dubuffet maintains that the meaning of a work of art is a function of the posture adopted by the artist during the process of creating it. It seems axiomatic that to appreciate art brut means to adopt as far as possible an approach in accordance with the attitudes that may be assumed to have been operative during its production. As an *alien* thing it cannot be assimilated via pre-existing faculties. One must, so to speak, develop new antennae through which to receive its message clearly. This is not easy: the autistic artist broadcasts on a very abstruse frequency. Yet some form of intuitive primitivism must be the ideal in our mode of reception if we are to make contact. At present we are not very close to this, and must content ourselves with an approximation of primitivism that, as a minimum virtue, avoids the obvious pitfalls of reflex comparison or valuation. In the future, one can only hope that creative empathy will form a basis for proper dialogue.

2 Artists outside culture

It's a feeling, you can *not* explain. You're born with it,
and it just comes out. That's *you*, and that's all about it.

Scottie Wilson

Adolf Wölfli 1864–1930

The remarkable artist Adolf Wölfli was born in Bern, Switzerland, in 1864. His father, a stonemason, became an alcoholic and abandoned his family; his mother was a woman of loose morals. The child lived in Bern until the age of eight, though nothing is known about this decisive period of his development. In 1872 his mother moved to the village of Schangnau, in the Emmenthal, where she fell ill. Her son was removed from her, and only learnt of her death some time afterwards. This must be counted as one of the shocks determining his subsequent psychic deterioration. As an orphan, Wölfli was left in the care of a succession of farming families, and led a harsh life marked by hunger and beatings. One day in 1876, he satisfied his sexual curiosity by uncovering a baby in its cradle; in later life he referred to the incident as a terrible sin for which he was obliged to suffer continual punishment.

While Wölfli was working as a farm-hand in Zäziwil, he fell violently in love with the farmer's daughter. The parents at once put a stop to the relationship, and Wölfli suffered a further psychic shock that plunged him into a profound depression. A friend tried to interest him in religion, but without success. Henceforth Wölfli was unable to resolve the tension between his instincts and external constraints, while the image of his beloved passed into his evolving private dream. After serving for a short period in the infantry, Wölfli returned to farm-work in the Bern region, and had three more unlucky amorous experiences: a brief encounter with the daughter of another employer, whom he promptly left; a short affair with a prostitute whom he all but married; and another with a widow, which, for unknown reasons, also foundered. Wölfli abandoned himself to a depraved mode of existence, fell ill with typhus for a time, and generally lived in a depressed condition. In the spring of 1880, whilst walking in the woods near Bern, he met a fourteen-year-old girl and tried to assault her. Though he managed to escape punishment for this offence, he was caught a few months later approaching a girl of five, and was committed to jail. Here he was treated as a dangerous prisoner capable of acts of great violence. While working with his fellow convicts one day, he had a vision of a shining presence which he identified as both the Holy Ghost and his 'little darling'.

On being released, Wölfli went back to Bern and worked as a gardener, a grave-digger and a delivery-clerk. His condition improved to the point where he was entrusted with the job of foreman on a building site, though he had to be relieved of this post because he was too demanding of his subordinates. For a time he became a regular church-goer, but attacks of violence soon came on again. The break with society was made definitive in 1895 when he was caught molesting a three-and-a-half-year-old child and, after a police enquiry, was sent for examination at the Waldau asylum

Adolf Wölfli *The Great Railroad of the Canyon of Anger* 1911
Collection de l'Art Brut, Paris, courtesy Jean Dubuffet

near Bern. Once interned, he was declared a schizophrenic and a danger to society, and never again left its walls.

Records of his early years in the asylum show that he was a patient who needed constant surveillance. He was subject to abrupt and ferocious outbursts, often breaking furniture and even attacking and wounding other patients. His moods ranged between manic zeal when he would saw wood with great energy, and bouts of depressive inertia in which he remained listlessly in the isolation of his cell. By 1897 he was having vivid hallucinations, imagining that those around him were his sworn enemies, and reacting by going berserk. His robust physique made these paroxysms very difficult to control. The records show they continued for several years, though the periods of calm gradually grew longer.

It was in about 1899 that Wölfli first showed artistic tendencies and soon he was spending most of his time in drawing, writing and composing music. These activities had all the signs of a compulsion; because they kept him quiet, the authorities encouraged them by supplying the necessary materials. In 1917 a particularly brutal outburst led to Wölfli's transfer to a cell in a wing well away from the other patients; here he stayed for the rest of his life in more or less complete isolation. The artist was concerned only that his piles of papers be transported intact, and soon settled down to a regular way of life. Though still pursued by hallucinations, he grew generally more stable, at the same time as his pictures grew more ordered. Receiving a weekly ration of pencils, paper and chewing-tobacco, he devoted himself absolutely to his art, hating to be interrupted and working away from dawn till dusk, transcribing without hesitation an endless flow of inspirations, which he would sometimes attribute to a divine source. 'There's so much to do here,' he would say. 'You'd never guess how you have to use your head so as not to forget anything. It would be enough to drive a body mad if he wasn't mad already.' Though he occasionally said a drawing was worthless, Wölfli was generally extremely proud of his pieces and marked some of them at prices mounting into millions of francs. His condition remained unchanged till his death from cancer in 1930, by which time the pile of papers in his cell was over two metres high.

The whole of Wölfli's creative output as an adult is devoted to relating the circumstances of his earliest childhood, which, he says, he was prevented from remembering for a while because of an illness contracted at the age of eight (the time when he was separated from his mother). He is thus recapitulating rather than inventing. His writings and drawings constitute a fantastic autobiography in which Wölfli casts himself in the role of 'Saint Adolf II', a child divinity in the care of an almighty God who acts as his guide in various adventures. Saint Adolf goes on endless journeys through the cosmos, plunging through infinite space, across mountains, oceans, jungles, and visiting gigantic cities full of great churches, banks and hotels, clustered with balconies, terraces and bell-towers. A repertoire of gods and goddesses often accompany him, as well as members of his family, including his descendants and a range of fiancées who satisfy his sexual needs. Among the animals that appear is the serpent, both a destructive and a life-giving force, being associated now with Satan as it curls around the tree of life, now with the Creator as its great coils encircle space and give a purchase on the infinite. The basic form of the snake, the ring, symbolizes the unbroken supremacy of Saint Adolf, who rules over a limitless world—as indeed Wölfli the artist ruled over a limitless imaginary kingdom. Yet Wölfli's mind contained signs of ambivalence. While able to affirm his absolute power, he could also express utter weakness and distress. Morgenthaler says that it was his nostalgia for his (presumably happy) early childhood that makes for this mixture of *folie de grandeur* and abject weakness. The complement of his manic-expansionist fantasies are depressive fantasies of destruction and punishment, based on the guilt attaching to the sinful act of 1876. These invariably take the form of a fall from a great height, as in the following account of a visit to the top of a tower that the young Saint Adolf makes on one of his outings. (My translation retains some of the eccentricities of the original text.)

> Whee had not been Up there more than ten minuttes: When I climbbed at a suittable place Its massieve and extraoordinarily luxurious balusstrade, became giddy and, fell from an altitude of circa 723 hours, straight down at sickkening speed: And I fell and I fell, till at last I was uttterly and totallly squashed and, splitt open upon the gigantic and extraoordinarily luxurious Sannta-Maria-Staar-Giant-Cathedral-Giant-Grand-Square. Aough!! Sobered down and dead: dead as a dooornail.

But the catastrophe is never final, for Saint Adolf is always being resurrected, on this occasion thanks to the divine intervention of Princess Sannta-Maria with her magic wand. These happy endings are always celebrated with great festivities, described in grandiloquent detail.

Wölfli's texts cover the back of his drawings, and sometimes suggest the inadequacy of the picture to convey the full impact of such monumentally epic events. The prose is an extraordinary mixture of the sublime and the crude, the magnificent and the burlesque. His large handwriting in old Germanic script loops across the paper interminably, weaving neologisms and piling up syntactic and semantic distortions in a frenzied rhythm of great inventiveness. Since ordinary language would be insufficient for his purpose, Wölfli runs words together, picks up sound associations and rhymes, makes puns and presses words into new meanings—'aphorism' denotes a precious stone, 'dilettante' a kind of star—and adds exotic words to his vocabulary—Ovianda, Alupka, Akmolinsk (some of these have been identified as Russian place-names picked up from an old atlas or the old numbers of a geographical magazine that are the only material Wölfli is known to have consulted). Robust interjections keep up the feeling of urgency as Wölfli spins his chains of words. Often the urge to apprehend the endless space that he has imagined finds expression in obsessive calculations of the riches that are his. Hundreds of figures cover his pages, and he even felt obliged to invent his own numerical system so as to encompass everything. After reaching a quadrillion, Wölfli goes off into his own numerals, each of which denotes a quantity ten times that of the preceding one—Regoniff, Suniff, Teratif, Unitif, Vidoniss, Weratif, Xylotif, and on up to Oberon, the only number that may not be surpassed, at the risk of total catastrophe. Dr Morgenthaler notes the mixed impression of enormity and exactness that is conveyed.

The quality of monstrous exactitude may also be found in the drawings. These are all done on paper, using black or colour pencils, occasionally incorporating pictures that Wölfli cut out of magazines when something caught his fancy. His designs were executed with remarkable skill: Wölfli never planned in advance, and never hesitated. Normally he would begin drawing at a given point on the edge of the sheet, and having drawn the border device, would add successive layers, moving inwards to the centre, and stopping only when the whole space was filled in—at which he would turn over and start his commentary. What Morgenthaler calls his *horror vacui* means that he left not a single empty space, if necessary adding disjointed sentences in the gaps in the picture.

Wölfli uses three main stereotyped motifs that are constantly reiterated, and serve as 'filler' material. These are the 'slugs', longish vague forms which are given an eye and an ear (somewhat like a comma and a full stop), the 'Hoptiquags', a variant on this, and above all the *Vögeli* (little birds), which sometimes look like a woman's high-heeled shoe, and bear the same 'eyes' and 'ears'. Morgenthaler sees the *Vögeli* not only as a convenient ornamental device, but also considers that its obsessional repetition may indicate a sexual significance, especially as it is often found as decoration on women's skirts in the early drawings. Spoerri suggests it could be explained in terms of Wölfli's shoe fetishism; and also points out that *vögeln* is a slang term for sexual intercourse. It may even be a phallic symbol.

Adolf Wölfli *St Adolf bitten in the leg by the serpent* 1921 verso showing Wölfli's
text describing the picture
Collection de l'Art Brut, Paris, courtesy Jean Dubuffet

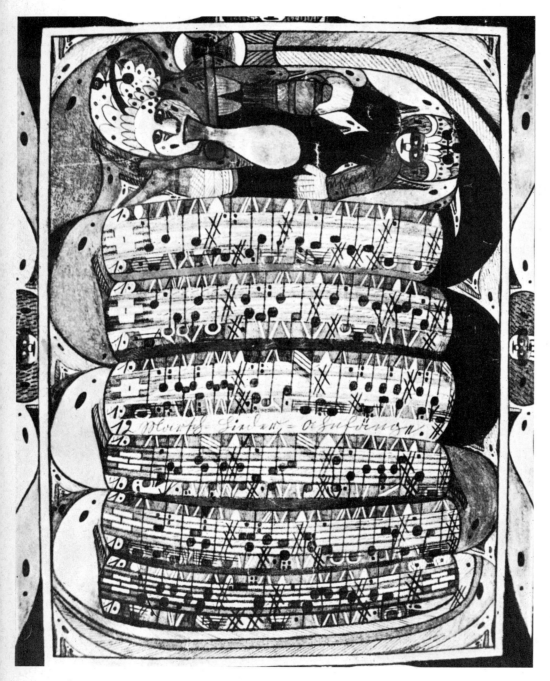

Adolf Wölfli *St Adolf bitten in the leg by the serpent* 1921 recto
Collection de l'Art Brut, Paris, courtesy Jean Dubuffet

The polyvalence of interpretations should remind one that the determinations of art like this originate at the undifferentiated levels of the unconscious, where all sorts of divergent meanings are suspended as equivalents in a way that is usually unacceptable to the differentiating mechanisms of the conscious mind. One might also recall Dubuffet's warning that it is meaningless to speak of total abstraction in art since decorative configurations are always potentially figurative.

Further devices can be mentioned: circles, crosses, little triangles, and what Wölfli calls his 'rings of bells' (discs linked by a thin line). This last resembles another fairly frequent motif, a stave on which are set musical notes. Wölfli did indeed have musical inclinations, priding himself on being a composer, and recording his tunes in an idiosyncratic notation that only he could decipher. He would perform marches, waltzes and mazurkas by humming down trumpets made out of rolled sheets of thick paper. Morgenthaler notes that he was attentive above all to the *rhythmic* aspects of music; and if actual sonorities are not possible, one can at least 'read' the scores inserted into his drawings as integral components of the visual rhythms.

The narrative content of the drawings is based on Wölfli's private mythology and hence contains a large number of characters, named either by labels adjacent to the figures, or in the commentary on the reverse of the drawing. It is important to note that these portraits are highly stylized. Full-length representation is comparatively rare, for Wölfli's main interest is in faces, and invariably the frontal view. Nearly always he exaggerates the size of the eyes, shading in the gap between eyelid and eyebrow to create the effect of a mask. Von Ries has pointed out the likelihood that Wölfli was influenced by the 'owl-face' motif found on pottery made at Heimberg, near Bern: the inventor of this motif was, interestingly enough, also schizophrenic, and several psychiatrists have indicated that excessive attention to the drawing of eyes is a characteristic shared by many, though by no means all, schizophrenic artists. Wölfli usually sets the pupils to one side, which gives the faces an expression of anxiety and emotional tension.

There is in fact no attempt to distinguish one face from another, except that male faces are given big handlebar moustaches. The 'portrait' is completed by a circle for the nose and a line for the mouth, with now and then a large tongue hanging out; ears are stuck on at either side, and hair is indicated either by sprays of colours emerging from the top of the head, or by a halo-like surround. Many heads are also equipped with a heavily stressed cross, that presumably indicates divine status. The rigidity of posture in Wölfli's figures establishes a general feeling of solemn ritual, that can become strangely moving if one learns from the commentary on the back that the scene depicted is in fact one of extreme violence—a fatal fall, or an execution. Ideally, of course, one should think of the individual work as the sum of the interacting elements of image and word.

Many drawings depict the countless gigantic cities that are scattered across Wölfli's mental universe. Henri-Pol Bouché suggests that a childhood experience of Wölfli's, in which he looked up at the Federal Parliament Buildings in Bern, looming up over the trees like some magic town, may have been the inspiration for the obsession. Certainly the clock-faces, which are a particularly noticeable feature of Bern, seem to have deep significance for him, possibly because they combine a semblance of human physiognomy with a set of 'magic' numerals. Buildings are rarely shown other than full-face, for Wölfli almost always ignores perspective. Together with fountains, balustrades, bridges and telegraph-poles, these serve to consolidate the rigid symmetry of the design. Against this are set disruptive curves, and indeed Wölfli's pictorial tensions seem to arise from the conflict between rigid straight lines or right angles, and more impulsive-seeming curves and circles, associated with the contours of rivers, curling railway lines, and the favourite image of the serpent, which in some pictures forms a mighty ring that enacts a gesture of encirclement suggestive of the artist's desire to embrace the totality of his cosmic and pictorial design.

Examination of Wölfli's drawings in their chronological sequence discloses a gradually evolving symmetry, a firmness and surety of design that, for the psychiatrist, betokens the gradual emergence of stable psychic structures out of the chaos of the personality collapse. Morgenthaler's description of this anticipates the theory of a restitution mechanism within the schizophrenic process such as has been propounded by, for example, Navratil. 'After Wölfli's psychotic collapse', writes Morgenthaler, 'it became evident that alongside the infinite expansion of the instinctual was something that persistently resisted it. This something was a kind of counter-instinct. It was the urge, innate in us all, to find some resting-point, the urge to emerge from turbulence into calm, to move from insecurity to stability, from fragmentation to unity, from boundlessness to limitation, from confusion to orderliness, from chaos to form.' That is, the urge towards the infinite or the gigantic that produced the monstrous richness of Wölfli's fantasies became slowly contained by a restraining urge that regulated and bound up the pictorial elements. It seems plausible that psychic stability was won by way of self-expression: little by little the artist was able to *realize*, in a manner more and more objectively fixed, that the coordinating factor in the turmoil of inspiration was his sense of self, of individual identity. The deployment of motifs about a central point towards which he gradually advanced, can be taken as reflecting a process of personality adjustment, a psychic exploration moving towards an affirmation of the unique self. The more Wölfli became Saint Adolf, the more he became assured of the power that lay 'at the center of alll this chaaos'. The controlling point in his cosmic design is this inner place of certainty, the centre of both pictorial square and cosmic circle, the figurative and emotional keystone of a divine plan which nothing could shake.

In the catalogue to the 1971 exhibition of Wölfli's work in Basel, Dieter Koepplin writes that 'there is no getting on to friendly terms with Wölfli's work, but only shock and wonderment.' Undeniably Wölfli's is an 'oblique equilibrium', in Spoerri's phrase, a balance gained at the expense of an autistic refusal of the norm. And yet the poet Rilke was willing to see in Wölfli's insane patterns a sign of Nature's intention to recover that which is aberrant so as to produce a new and harmonious synthesis. Singularly disproportionate in terms of what some fancy is the superior symmetry of sanity, Wölfli's throbbing imagery issues forth from his isolated cell to voice an arresting declaration of imaginative independence that puts in serious doubt the adequacy of collective rationality.

See also cover and illustrations pages 25, 43, 50.

Clarence Schmidt 1898–

Born in New York City, Clarence Schmidt moved in 1920 to the Catskill Mountain region about a hundred miles to the north. For many years he worked as a plasterer and stonemason, building many of the walls that line the roadsides around Woodstock. In the thirties he began to construct a log cabin to live in, choosing a wooded site on the slope of the Ohayo Mountain. When this was finished, Schmidt did not stop but continued his single-handed work, moving on up the mountain, adding room after room. Some thirty years later the building had become a seven storey house with at least thirty-five rooms, interconnected by labyrinthine passageways.

Built of rough-cut wood picked up at the local sawmill, Schmidt's House looms out from the mountainside, thrusting jagged struts and ramshackle spires against the sky. An array of windows covers the face of the cliff where chambers were dug out as much as forty feet into the earth. Within, the rooms are wired for coloured lights, and are crammed with innumerable pieces of junk, mostly wrapped in aluminium foil to catch the light— coat-hangers, old shoes, dried ferns, piano parts, coffee-pots, antlers. What in other dwellings constitutes the attic has here taken over the whole house. Dolls and plastic flowers set in niches create the effect of little 'shrines' inside the grottoes, and Schmidt even added stained glass by coating some of the windows with a translucent paint mixture. Room after room is thus decorated with society's leftovers, which this hermit has lovingly integrated into his imaginative world. Bits of cars and broken household appliances are joined with bits of nature, such as the branch of a live tree that was incorporated into the structure of the building.

Outside, Schmidt's Garden extends up and around the House to constitute the total environment in which he lives. Multi-level paths cover several acres, winding about in a forest of tar-covered trees, piled stones, bedsteads, broken clocks, old cutlery, hurricane-lamps, lawn-mowers, bicycle frames, coils of garden hose, seashells, and countless other objects, many of which are painted or set in plaster. A stool is nailed to the top of a post; death-masks on a tree-trunk form a weird totem pole. Old mirrors are nailed up everywhere to catch the light and the reflection of the trees and the objects wrapped in sparkling foil. The integration of the man-made and the natural is complete. Nature is involved, made welcome, and adds her own touches to the work—real flowers sprout amongst the plastic ones, birds fly in and out of the junk, rain and wind rot the woodwork and attack the paint. The changing seasons affect the work in different ways: 'I love to see the light on it,' muses Schmidt, 'the reflections and shadows keep changing. The pieces are wonderful in the moonlight, and at sunset, and after a snowfall.'

Clarence Schmidt Garden

Clarence Schmidt Garden

The artist is well aware that what he has made is a challenge to art as it is normally understood: 'There's more art here than in all the museums in the entire country! Forget the Pyramids and the Mona Lisa!' He insists that there is nothing else like it in the world, and he is perfectly right inasmuch as his work bears the imprint of his unique personality. Though happy to greet visitors, especially if they present him with something that he can use, Schmidt glories in being off the beaten track, calling himself 'the original hippie', affirming his distinct separateness, his identity with a private domain that he has set against what surrounds it. And yet his work is not conceived as solipsistic escapism, but as an appeal to the rest of mankind. His attitude reflects an almost utopian concern for humanity, as is shown in the credo he has painted up over his mail-box: 'My mirrored hope—one for all and all for one.' When asked about his motives in creating such a mammoth work, Schmidt will reply in somewhat grandiose terms:

'I guess I did it to help humanity—to bring some comfort and pleasure to people. All of my life I've dreamed of creating something that would live forever in the minds of men.' The altruistic motive is hard to separate from the more self-involved one.

In a letter to a friend, Schmidt has evoked what he calls 'lofty generalities captured and firmly held', expressing his eagerness for the moment when 'a treasure triumphs and kills the dragon', for an end to the conflict between felicity and devastation, in which he hopes 'against hope that felicity may reign'. Not long ago Schmidt experienced the reign of devastation. For years he had been harrassed by neighbours who could not tolerate his cheerful non-conformism and who were afraid that the value of their properties would be affected by the junk and the odd visitors it attracted. One neighbour even claimed Schmidt's land, accusing him of being a squatter; ownership was difficult to determine, as the area had never been properly surveyed. Finally most of Schmidt's House was destroyed in a raging fire that one suspects did not start accidentally. Losing the results of a lifetime's work, Schmidt merely shrugged and set to work once more. At his present age, he has been unable to progress fast, although he recently wrapped a whole spinney at the foot of the hill to form a little metal forest.

Hitting spontaneously upon so many of the experimental devices of the avant-garde of this century—*objets trouvés*, assemblages, environments, wrappings—Schmidt has created something that must be situated well beyond the territory of *art culturel*. Built from tangible materials, his work reflects the thoughts and emotions of its creator: it can readily be conceived as a kind of 'ideal palace'—something that 'lives in the mind' as much as in materiality. This might be one consolation for its having been partly destroyed. Alternatively one might argue that this was just another stage in a ceaseless sequence of transformations. Was it not logical that there should be the intervention of fire after that of the other three elements? Schmidt's work reveals new notions of what art *can be*—something non-rational, organic and impermanent, as are the forms of nature or the inner processes of the psyche. It exemplifies an art sublimely indifferent to the 'frozen' values of organized culture: a reappraisal of what society has designated as obsolescent, Schmidt's creation triumphs in its continuing evolution, voicing an eloquent homage to the principle of Change.

See also illustration page 129.

Heinrich Anton Müller 1865–1930

Born in Boltigen, Switzerland, in 1865, Heinrich Anton M. lived for most of his life in the French-speaking canton of Vaud. He worked in the vineyards, and had a wife and children. In 1903 he invented an ingenious machine for trimming the vines, but was deprived of the benefits of this invention when it was commercially exploited by other hands. The frustration this caused was probably the main motive for his engaging upon a process of systematic refusal of normal life that, despite medical treatment, led to his internment at the age of forty-one as a mental patient in a hospital at Münsingen. After a restless period of hallucinations and delusions, he had by 1912 settled down to a steady existence devoted to his private activities. He dug a deep hole in the hospital garden, and spent a lot of time inside it. He made a hammock out of branches, and a number of strange machines, possibly in an attempt to discover the secret of perpetual motion. He drew a good deal upon large sheets of thick wrapping paper, sometimes roughly sewn together, using a big black pencil and white chalk softened with saliva; these pictures were used to decorate his room. Though he depicts things such as farm animals, people, trees and bicycles which are manifestly drawn from his ordinary experience, the deformations which he imposes upon them—probably intentionally—place them at a considerable remove

Heinrich Anton M. *Three women in a wheelbarrow* 1917–22
Collection de l'Art Brut, Paris, courtesy Jean Dubuffet

from normality. Heinrich Anton's art is thus one of deliberate grotesqueness: his goats sprout root-like claws, and his human figures secrete disquieting shadows, their aberrant contours containing as it were a dual personality, both light and dark. Apart from writing some rhythmical prose pieces, he also introduced calligraphy into his pictures, carefully inscribing phrases around or inside the outlines of his figures to produce weird convolutions of letter and image that have a half-amusing, half-frightening quality. In 1924, he gave up drawing for a year, and then resumed once more, producing a series of drawings in a new style, using coloured pencils; as for example *The fly-man and the snake*, with a human figure whose outline trembles like the lines on a seismograph and whose facial expression suggests mingled surprise and resignation. In 1926 Heinrich Anton busied himself with erecting a large 'telescope' in the garden, through which, for hours on end, he carried out observations upon a kind of totemic assemblage he had made out of stones and other materials. He died in 1930.

Heinrich Anton M. *The fly-man and the snake* 1925–7
Collection de l'Art Brut, Paris, courtesy Jean Dubuffet
See also illustration page 31.

Pascal Maisonneuve 1863–1934

Pascal-Désir Maisonneuve was a second-hand dealer in Bordeaux, and a great collector of strange objects, which he hated having to sell. His father, a mosaicist, had taught him his trade, and at one time his son enjoyed a certain 'respectable' reputation as the result of his skilled restoration of Gallo-Roman mosaics for the local museums. But he was essentially a man of impulsive character and derisive bent, an individualist who loved to challenge authority. Once, after he had been sued by a priest who had asked him to clear out his attic but had not given him permission to dispose of the highly valuable reliquary that had inadvertently been left there, Maisonneuve responded by hanging up a bucket at the door of his shop with a notice inviting passers-by to dip into the holy water. He claimed that priests came on bended knee to implore him to remove it, but he would not give way. He also kept a talking parrot, which he trained to cry out revolutionary slogans: when the police protested, he coolly ran up the red flag on his roof. At the age of sixty-four he collected together several cases full of shells and fragments of coral, and over a period of a year amused himself with putting them together with the help of plaster to form a series of about fifteen shell-faces. The intention was to satirize well-known international figures such as the German Crown Prince and Queen Victoria, though there are other grotesque portraits—a Chinaman, a Tartar, and the devil. In these faces, the caricatural impulse, exploiting incongruous material, attains a pitch of extravagant derision that both mocks actual political figures and pokes a tongue at the rules of conventional representation.

Pascal Maisonneuve *The Crown Prince* 1927–8
Collection de l'Art Brut, Paris, courtesy Jean Dubuffet

Scottie Wilson 1890–

Many naïve painters take pleasure in the world they inhabit. Brick by brick, leaf by leaf, artists such as Louis Vivin and Adolf Dietrich plot the minutiae of their surroundings so meticulously that their pictures become mannered representations of a reality that seems too clear-cut, too clean. Pictures of this kind appear more as exemplary 'fair copies' of the real, rather than dynamic transfigurations of it; they are not really inventive. Accepted conventions of representation, usually of the most academic sort, provide a comforting support for those who dare not break away from the external model, or who do not admit to themselves that the external model pure and simple is not a valid incentive to 'create'. It may be that naïve painting becomes less depressingly conformist to the extent that the individual artist adopts a posture of refusal, and declines to foster a passive mode of looking at things. For the innocent eye sees things much more clearly when it does not look outwards through the naïve peephole, but when it turns inwards upon the world of imagined forms, and what André Breton calls *le modèle intérieur*. At this point it is possible to speak of 'raw' creation, of a fertile and authentic primitivism.

The majority of the cases featured in Oto Bihalji-Merin's book *Das naïve Bild der Welt* (1959) appear to belong to the conventional type of naïve artist that I have described. It therefore comes as something of an embarrassment for Bihalji-Merin to be faced with an artist who all too clearly escapes his classification (one wonders why he got himself into this position). Coming to the work of Scottie Wilson, he is obliged to make a telling distinction: 'If the main characteristic of the naïf is his earnest indebtedness to reality, if materiality and the Great Real experience their rediscovery in the art of the naïf, Scottie Wilson has severed the umbilical cord that links him with the visible things of this world.' The admission is that Scottie's refusal to compromise with external facts places him at once outside the ranks of the passive copyists and in the much more exclusive category of those who have genuine imaginative independence, those who, to adopt a phrase coined by Yrjö Hirn, have 'faith in the reality of the unreal'.

Robert 'Scottie' Wilson was born in Glasgow in 1890. His family was working-class and poor. The few details mentioned by the artist about his childhood bear upon his four brothers, of whom three were 'bad', and only one, Frank, is remembered with affection. His father was an assistant to a taxidermist, and used to stuff fish, birds and other creatures, a fact to which Mervyn Levy in part ascribes the catalyptic, trance-like quality of the bird and animal forms in Scottie's pictures. As a child, Scottie played in the streets, or in a park whose brown-stone fountain and birds may have provided the original seeds for the 'alternative' world of his drawings.

Sometimes he got to see animals at the zoo or the circus. At the age of nine, Scottie ran away from school, an event of major importance in his conception of his development. 'Perhaps I can see as clearly as I do because I ran away from school', he chuckles. Jean Dubuffet responds to his insistence on his lack of formal education by arguing that Scottie's wisdom and insight are precisely a function of his having escaped the conditioning process of an imposed education. That Scottie cannot write more than his name, and reads with difficulty, does not mean that he is a fool, but rather that he lays proper stress on speech and independent thought. Here is an artist who has no indebtedness to cultural art and indeed knows next to nothing of it: he is not even interested. His is the independence of the man who refuses to sign the socio-cultural contract, and any 'culture' he has is what he himself has elaborated by dint of meditating upon the circumstances of his life.

After a period in which he made his way by selling patent medicines in the Glasgow streets with his elder brother, Scottie joined the Scottish Rifles at the age of sixteen, and went to serve in India and South Africa. Here he made enough money to buy his discharge, and returned to Britain. When war broke out, he joined up and fought on the Western Front. Afterwards he returned to a life as street trader in Glasgow and London. He had a stall in the Caledonian Market, and then a shop in the Edgware Road, selling anything he could lay his hands on to bring in an income. After a short time in Canada, he decided in about 1931 to return there more or less permanently, submitting to what he indicates to be the inexplicable necessity of his life as mapped out by some unnamed agency; though it seems likely that he emigrated in response to an extremely accurate intuition of the horrors that were to beset Europe as the thirties wore on. He moved about the country as a general trader, and at last took a shop in Yonge Street, Toronto, where he dealt in cut-glass novelties and bought up old fountain-pens so as to make money out of their gold nibs. He acquired a large table with a thick cardboard top on which to put his radio set. One day he was listening to some music and inspecting one of his finds, a pen that he describes as 'looking like a bulldog, with a nib as thick as my finger'. He felt it too magnificent a trophy to break up. Suddenly he dipped it into a bottle of ink to try it out, doodling upon the surface of the table. This absorbing activity went on for two days, at the end of which time the tabletop was entirely covered in complicated designs. The inspiration appears to have been entirely spontaneous, even compulsive. A friend saw the table and congratulated him on his ability. Scottie went out to buy exercise books, drawing pads and cheap coloured pencils, and very soon drawing had become his principle activity in life. He sold his

Scottie Wilson *Curiosity* 1941
Brook Street Gallery, London

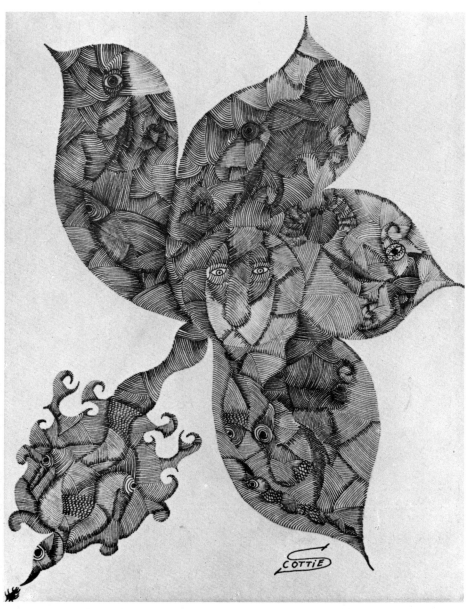

Scottie Wilson *Dream house* 1946
Brook Street Gallery, London

shop and moved to Vancouver, where he lived in the Chinese quarter
in a room whose walls he covered with drawings in lieu of wallpaper.

The drawings of this period are his most impressive. They consist of
shapes filled with hundreds of lines traced by the pen, line upon line applied
under the varying pressure of an unsophisticated hand. The variations of
stroke, lost in engraved versions of his work, constitute Scottie's personal
'handwriting', his own delicate yet robust touch. Here pulse the inarticulate
tremors of expression that then release a whole pageant of faces and animals.
Some of the faces are clownish self-portraits; others, grotesque and sinister,
represent 'Greedies'—the despised forces of evil. Many of these are built
up into menacing 'totem-poles' that are a distinct and original invention,
despite the comparison that has been made between them and the Indian
totem-poles that Scottie saw in Vancouver Park. One totem-pole drawing
was done on thick paper, fifteen feet by four. Other motifs are the diving

ducks and frogs which he loved to watch in Vancouver. But like the stylized fish and trees that proliferate in his work, these externals are sucked into the swirl of a truly creative inner vision. Of course one 'recognizes' them as birds and fish; but, as is the case with any genuinely imaginative art, their essential virtue lies in what they reveal to us of a source that we cannot pretend to know. Such creatures thus lead us away from the familiar to a new world whose 'spatial' limitations do not correspond to its actual vitality, athrob as it is with the struggle between darkness and light, destruction and purity. Dubuffet considers these drawings to be, of all those he knows, 'the most highly charged and cerebral, the most disconcerting and fascinating'.

At this point, it may be interesting to give a transcription of a dream that Scottie related to me, and which clearly moved him. The setting is Vancouver, near the Harbour:

> It was one of those dreams you can't forget—full of music. They were all coming over the hill, the people ballet-dancing over the hill. And I was down there selling my designs—all on rice-tissue paper—and the music was playing and the people coming over the hill, all going to meet the boat.
>
> Suddenly the music stopped. I looked down the pit to see if my stall was there: it had disappeared. I felt very sad. If anything's real, that was real.

The immediacy of this dream account expresses at once the sense of the *reality* of the imagined world, while at the same time showing a poignant awareness of its fragility. Creative work is associated with feelings of confidence and plenitude; but this is menaced by the urgent necessities of everyday life, that break in on the dream-world and disrupt its subtle harmonies. Silence and foreboding gloom are what remain once the dream is shattered.

Scottie remained in Canada during the Second World War. If at first he had refused to make money out of his drawings, and only consented to give them away to people that he knew would appreciate them, he was in time obliged to earn his living through them, since they had become his sole activity. Yet he avoided actually selling them, preferring to organize travelling shows and setting up exhibitions on hired premises such as old shops or cinema foyers. In 1945 he returned to Britain, and put on shows there, in an old wallpaper shop on the front at Scarborough and a dance hall in Aberdeen, where he did very well. There were times when these ventures ended sadly, and those who had paid their sixpence to see the show were not moved to donate anything further. Not long after his return from Canada, art experts and London gallery owners managed to persuade Scottie to let them show his pieces in more glamorous surroundings, and in a more commercially viable manner. His work, after all, was gaining a reputation. Shows were thus put on in London galleries, and still continue. In 1947 Scottie was featured at the major surrealist exhibition in Paris, and in 1952 at the large exhibition of fantastic art in Basle, the particularity of his works eluding final assimilation by these contexts. In time, Scottie met Dubuffet, who acquired much early work for the Compagnie de l'Art Brut. Later, Scottie was persuaded to do a large mural for a Basle bank, and to design a whole table service for an English ceramic firm. In his commercial dealings, he managed to remain untouched by the atmosphere of condescension and profiteering; never a victim of the fake admiration poured on him, he always knew that his attendance at cocktail parties in the galleries was by way of 'decoration', and from time to time would react to commercialism by selling off pictures in the street at a pound or so a time, to the great dismay of the gallery-owners who had priced his pieces at two hundred and fifty times as much! Scottie ultimately preferred showing his work in an old bus in Cardiff, or on the front at Margate, with one-man publicity in the form of hand-drawn posters and an old record-player to attract attention. Of the working-class audience he drew in at Blackpool, he remarks appreciatively: '*They're* the intellect, you know.'

It may seem remarkable that an artist whose works have been acquired by the Museum of Modern Art in New York, the Musée de l'Art moderne in Paris, the Tate Gallery in London, and museums in major cities in Canada and Switzerland, insists on living alone in a dull back room in a house in Kilburn, North-West London. Resisting any change in his established way of life, Scottie follows a simple routine, working slowly and painstakingly at a plain table cluttered with coloured pencils. His pictures have now lost the sinister qualities of the Canadian days. The battle between the 'Greedies' and the 'Clowns' has been won, pictorially at least, by the latter. The scenes now depicted attain a utopian serenity: they consist of bright patterns with peaceful villages amid trees where birds and butterflies play, or magical *châteaux* with calm swans and flowers. The innocent eye has finally imposed the vision of a totally innocent world. Only in Scottie's talk does there persist the old antagonism between corruption and wisdom, evil and good. Frequently he will launch into long diatribes against those people who manufacture hate and jealousy, who put out propaganda to deceive the common man, or who simply wrap ideas up in stifling cocoons of fine talk ('blah-blah-blah'). The newspaper and his ever-present radio set provide plenty of material for his analysis of a corrupt and frightening world. And yet his bitter castigations seem always to be relieved by a different mood, in a progression from acrimony to hope that exactly reverses the order of moods conveyed by his Vancouver dream. The indictment of 'this rotten world', this 'cock-eyed so-called civilization' is followed by a moving statement of his confidence in the possibility one day—perhaps as much as a hundred and fifty years from now, but certainly *sometime*—of a regeneration of mankind, an entry into a new order of things in which a wise simplicity will obtain in human relations, and a true 'civilization' will emerge. In the meantime, Scottie lives on in accordance with his beliefs, regretting only that he has not met the few great men he admires: Rabbie Burns, Einstein, Charlie Chaplin—and accepting life as it has been mapped out for him: 'It's all writ out for you.' Above all he is conscious of his individuality, his inexplicable uniqueness, succinctly expressed in his jaunty yet serious explanation of his life and art: 'that's *you* and that's all about it.'

See also illustrations pages 48, 122, 124.

Johann Knüpfer 1866–?

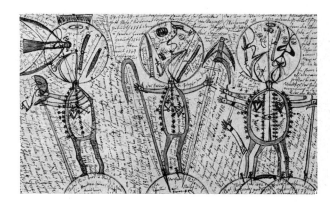

Johann Knüpfer
Three Figures
Prinzhorn collection,
Heidelberg

Johann Knüpfer was born in 1866, in a village in the Odenwald in Germany. His father, who may have been subject to religious mania, died at an early age. Knüpfer first worked as a baker's apprentice, did military service, and then took various factory jobs, ending up as a plumber in a factory. At the age of thirty he was a quiet and reserved worker, still living with his brother and his mother. In 1895 his mother died, and the shock obviously provoked his subsequent mental disorders. Knüpfer now got married, against his will as he later claimed, and soon abandoned his quiet, diligent way of life, changing jobs again and again, drinking, and quarrelling violently with his wife. Symptoms of a persecution mania began to build up: the drink his wife handed him was poisoned, smoke blowing out of the fire was chloroform. Knüpfer felt himself to be a martyr, and had visions of Christ the Saviour, who would alert him to the dealings of his tormentors. In 1902 he inflicted a wound on himself with a knife and was brought to an asylum. It was early in the twenties that Prinzhorn studied his drawings at Heidelberg. The date of Knüpfer's death is not available.

As Prinzhorn notes, the picture is that of mild schizophrenia lacking an acute phase. Knüpfer's thought disorder was such that he could interpret all kinds of minor incidents so that they fitted in with his delusional mood, which was thus unshakeable. In his religious megalomania he saw himself as the persecuted martyr, the slaughtered lamb, whose pride was to suffer even more than Christ had done. Soon after entering the asylum, Knüpfer began to draw, and many of his pictures are of a mannikin representing Christ the Saviour, or perhaps Knüpfer himself, inasmuch as he associated himself with the saviour's role. The face in these pictures is in the form of a circle which is at the same time a radiant sun, an ostensory, and even a clock-face on which the numbers go up to twenty-four or even higher.

Here Knüpfer has invented a complex image, several associations being superimposed on the one shape to create a dazzling and polyvalent 'icon'. In one picture the face appears encircled in the bell of a bassoon. There is a good deal of repetition, as in the recurrent motif of the heart, seen either through the transparent bodies (as in Catholic images of the Sacred Heart) or placed freely elsewhere in the picture. Numerals play some sort of 'magical' role, and writing is also integral to the total picture. The tenor of Knüpfer's texts, which fill up space between the contours of the objects and were added by turning the page different ways round, is hieratic and Biblical, with some joking asides. Apart from the religious drawings, there are some that illustrate childhood memories of life on a farm. These often comprise pedantic ground-plans with stereotyped geese, rabbits and farmers. One of the most impressive elements is the stylized, quasi-heraldic bird that is included in most pictures. Clearly there is an affinity here, for Knüpfer is reported as saying that he was able to understand bird language. These birds have outspread wings, and are pursued from time to time by men with knives and fearsome shotguns. Occasionally the birds have human faces, a hint that Knüpfer identified them as symbols of his martyrdom. They may also suggest angels with radiant smiles who soar up joyously to escape the earthbound hunters.

Johann Knüpfer
Composition with birds
Prinzhorn collection,
Heidelberg

See also illustration page 132.

Guillaume 1893–

Guillaume was born in Saint-Gaudens, in the south-west of France, and at the age of fourteen left school to become the apprentice to his father, a cabinet-maker, who taught him how to design and construct furniture. A serious and sensitive boy, he hated any disorderliness and showed an almost pathological concern for his personal appearance, constantly polishing his shoes and checking that his buttons were properly sewn on. When his father incurred severe gambling debts and the business began to go downhill, Guillaume's hostile remonstrations revealed deep feelings of anxiety and guilt. In 1913 he left home on an impulse to join the army. During the war he was wounded in Belgium, caught malaria in Salonika, and was finally captured during an enemy attack on the Western Front in which he persisted in firing wildly against impossible odds. In 1919 he was released from prison-camp and returned to his family; but, unable to come to terms with his father, he soon left again to become a customs-official in Metz. In 1924 he married, but his mania for perfection—meals cooked just so, every object in its proper place—and his narcissistic devotion to his own appearance made conjugal life very painful. All the same, Guillaume had strong feelings for his wife, and when, in 1925, he left to take up a new post at Urdos, on the understanding that she would follow three months later, he plunged into a crisis of jealousy, asserting that she was betraying him with his best friend. The psychic pressures were such that, failing any other outlet, he directed his violence against himself, cutting his throat with a knife. Not serious enough to be fatal, the act may be construed as a symbolic severing of contact with reality, the confirmation of a commitment to a substitute consciousness of things. Guillaume was hospitalized and now gave way to melancholic fantasies revolving around his wife, his one link with the outside world. He imagined she had an illegitimate daughter, whom he saw peeping at him through the windows. For a while, his condition improved, and the doctors allowed him to return to his wife for a trial period: but his delirium was sufficiently entrenched to absorb the influence of the real, using it as raw material for further fantasies. Confrontation with objective facts only stimulated the mechanisms of deformation. One day Guillaume went berserk, throwing away his father's watch and his mother's engagement ring, and menacing his wife with a loaded pistol; he was soon removed to an asylum in Toulouse, where his wife, who appears to have remained very loyal to him, took a job as nurse. After another attack on her, Guillaume refused to see her for two years, and by the time he encouraged her visits once more, all his aggression had been channelled into his fantasies and was no longer associated with the actual woman, towards whom he henceforth manifested a polite indifference.

Guillaume *The 'Provence', an animated drawing* 1946
Collection de l'Art Brut, Paris, courtesy Jean Dubuffet

In 1935, after a quarrel with one of the male nurses, Guillaume took revenge by drawing a caricature of him which was much appreciated by the other patients. Encouraged by this success, he began to draw assiduously, finding that artistic activity tranquillized him and guided his energies in a productive direction. Using different materials at different periods—inks, pencils, chemical fluids such as tincture of iodine, and sometimes gouache— he established a working method. His drawings are always based on newspaper or magazine illustrations, whose outlines he transcribes with pencil or pen. Though the first stage of composition is arguably still attached to an objective model, one imagines that the process of deformation has begun, and the vestiges of attachment do not survive for long. After obtaining the preliminary 'copy', Guillaume as it were empties the figure of all original content, and treats it as an empty receptacle in which to collect his own ideas. The colours he uses are arbitrary and unrealistic, usually pale pinks and inscrutable blacks, dream-like colours that correspond to a purely detached vision. His obsessive meticulousness is evinced in an attentiveness to a clean finish. He relies on a whole array of instruments—dividers, ruler, compass, pens, many of them made with his own hands and ritualistically conserved in a special box.

The scenes Guillaume depicts—plunging ships, spooky castles, swooping birds, leaping tigers—are animated by what Dr Jean Dequeker, in his admirable monograph on Guillaume, calls a 'lyrical wind'. Dequeker goes on to describe this 'strange world possessed of a fantastic beauty composed of splashes spreading forth, tormented emblems, blurred streaks, darts of flame'. The fanatic sharpness of the lines accentuates the singularity of a realm of convulsive forms that are bound by the authority of a unified vision. The title and signature at the bottom of each picture form arabesques that are equally sharp and wild.

Dequeker states that Guillaume used what little of external reality he was still prepared to recognize as a point of reference or an alibi: 'Everywhere he seizes upon morphological analogies, distant resemblances, in the haze of external representations.' This is far from saying that he copied the exterior model. Obliged to seek protection from his conflicts, Guillaume's 'madness' was a carefully organized sabotaging of any holds that reality might still have upon him. Rather than reproduce the world that had caused him anguish and uncertainty, Dubuffet argues, he laid claim to a new world in which his emotional problems could be resolved, an invented world in which the antagonisms of the beautiful and the ugly, the pleasant and the horrifying, would be eliminated. For him this personal world was purified of all turbulence: his pinks and blacks are the colours of a dispassionate region where he could feel secure from emotion, his exact lines the armature of an artistic structure whose beauty lay in its affective frigidity. After about 1949 Guillaume gave up his pictures, and made furniture, aluminium rings, and a few quaint toys, such as a wooden aeroplane and a revolver with a toothbrush barrel. This would appear to be a return to the tangible world, but it may well be that his confidence had grown to the extent that these apparent 'objects' were for their maker pure mental products.

See also illustrations page 123.

Bogosav Živković *Monastery on a wild goat*
Reproduced from *Bogasav Živković* by
O. Bihalji-Merin, by kind permission of
Jugoslavija Editions

Bogosav Živković 1920–

Bogosav Živković was born of peasant stock in the Yugoslav village of Leskovac. As a child he took sheep and pigs to pasture; he then became a farmhand and in 1942 began work as a furrier. During the war he three times underwent torture at the hands of collaborators, from which he received spinal injuries which still trouble him. After the war, he moved to Belgrade, being employed in a furriers' cooperative until 1956, when, for health reasons, he had to take a job as porter in a ministerial building. He suffered from insomnia, and, when he did sleep, had terrible nightmares caused by his wartime experience. In 1957 he dreamt one night that he was pursued by a slimy snake that wrapped itself round a man and stifled him. On awaking, he sprang out of bed and without having really regained consciousness, struck at a log with his axe. The log was shaped into his first work, a man with a snake. The creative act offered a means of projecting the nightmare and thus severing it from himself: by externalizing his horror, he exorcised it. Ever since, he has kept a carving of a snake under a chest in his bedroom, a monster no longer feared but rendered familiar.

Živković loves wood and always chooses the hardest he can find—cherry, walnut and oak. He takes gnarled trunks or roots, steams them to get rid of any insects or grubs and to make the wood dry and hard; then he works upon it with an axe and a sharp knife, finally rubbing the carving with another piece of hard wood to leave a polished surface. The knots and branches of his trunks suggest forms which the carver 'releases', grave faces, plants and hybrid beasts which grow in and out of one another. They emerge and yet never fully emerge from the wood, which retains its essential character as brute matter. Often the figures are set one above the other in a way that tempts one to draw the comparison with Indian totem-poles; in fact Živković knows nothing of North American primitive art, nor indeed of any art beyond the folk arts of his region. It cannot be denied that these have influenced his work, but they have done so only to a limited degree: his independence from objective models is sufficiently pronounced for him to earn a legitimate place in this book.

See also illustrations page 130.

August Klotz 1864–?

Born in 1864, the son of a well-to-do and domineering German businessman, August Klotz was a reserved and uncommunicative child. After military service, he worked in Belgium and England in the export trade, and from 1891 worked for his father's agency as a wine-salesman. He was an elaborately polite and phlegmatic person, who coped well with his work and was popular with women. Then, after an illness, he became extremely taciturn, had depressive guilt feelings, and took to drink. He began to hear voices insulting and accusing him; one day he tried to commit suicide by knifing himself in the stomach. After his internment in an asylum in 1903, he remained depressed and withdrawn, then began to show signs of megalo-mania, making himself out to be Christ and pointing to his stomach-scar as authentication of his sufferings on the cross. His mood would switch rapidly between sullenness and frenzy. As his auditory hallucinations grew worse, he became exceedingly irritable. He said he could see devils grinning up at him in the patterns of the carpet, and one day he was found making a picture on the carpet in smeared fat. Klotz composed interminable letters to the authorities, complaining about annoyances. In time he moved from an acute phase to a confirmed schizophrenic condition in which his personality showed a systematic coherence, albeit of a peculiar kind.

Developing potentialities set free on his withdrawal from reality, Klotz elaborated a number of highly personal 'systems' including a colour alphabet and a chart of analogies between different sorts of substances, chemicals, plants, smells, etc. It might be argued that tables of this sort, based on no external criteria, constitute a deliberately *unreal* armature for the new psychic system. Self-confirming occultation seems of the essence. A second alphabet correlated letters not only with colours but with numbers too, and allowed Klotz to 'add up' the letters of each word and so arrive at a quasi-cabbalistic quantification of his sentences, a sort of arithmetical totting-up of meaning.

In his drawings, Klotz followed an alternately passive and active method. He would begin to draw without any model in mind, using a pencil and occasionally taking a ruler or a flat stone as something to draw round and so 'get going'. After drawing automatically and playfully for a while he would look at what he had done, and give it a conscious interpretation. After emendations, he would proceed to draw aimlessly again. Thus the pictures took shape as accretions of unforeseen shapes on which the secondary process of conscious ordering was only applied at separate moments. Many images are conglomerations of pictorial elements such as faces, clouds, fish, birds and the like, which combine in a way reminiscent of the con-densation mechanism analysed by Freud. Superimposition or counter-change produce 'multi-layered' images, and Klotz shows a spontaneous talent in exploiting the double meaning of shapes. His picture *Wurmlöcher* (*Worm-holes*) shows a head in profile with wavy hair that incorporates fingertips, worms, and caterpillar heads. Another part of the head juxtaposes nuns and flamingoes. Klotz's delight in these obscure yet suggestive games is evident from the way he recapitulates a decisive formula once he has hit upon it. On the back of the pictures figure long explanations of an irrational character, in which words are subjected to similar combinations and contaminations. Klotz has a particular fondness for mammoth compound nouns, for example the word *Halmdolchfischgradtropfeneiweiss* ('Stalk-dagger-fish-bone-drop-egg-white'), which sounds like a synopsis for a nonsense story, though its 'free' associations doubtless had significance for its author. A marked taste for what Prinzhorn calls 'suspended ambiguity' leads Klotz to coin self-contradictory statements that reflect a schizophrenic desire to have things both ways at once. A touch of humour is apparent in the title of one picture, *Chimney-sweep-snow in spring*, which conflates the two contrasts black/white and winter/spring. Such 'convulsive' inventions make sense only if taken in via our non-differentiating faculties, which work best in the state of daydreaming or what we are wont to call, in our embarrassment, our absent-minded moments.

August Klotz *Wurmlöcher* (*Worm-holes*)
Prinzhorn collection, Heidelberg

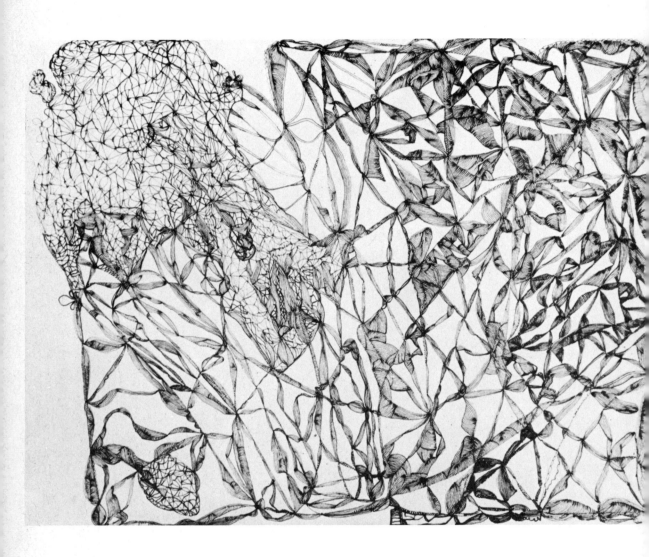

Laure Pigeon Drawing dated 2 August 1935
Collection de l'Art Brut, Paris, courtesy Jean Dubuffet

Laure Pigeon 1882–1965

Laure was born in 1882 in Val d'Izé, Brittany. As her mother died soon after, she was brought up by a strict grandmother. In 1911, against the family's wishes, she married a prosperous dentist, with whom she lived happily for twenty years. In 1933, Laure discovered her husband was having an affair, and left him. Her attachment to him had been deep, and this separation was a profound emotional shock. For ten years, Laure lived in a boarding-house, where a friend introduced her to spiritualism. It was at this point, at the age of about fifty-one, that Laure started to draw, at first under some form of astrological inspiration, as is indicated by allusions to the planets in the titles of her earliest work. The early drawings consist of areas of uncertain shape swathed in ribbons and curls traced in ink. There is no evident attempt at representation, and, as it is possible that Laure rarely lifted her pen from the paper, the composition can be taken as constituting space 'filled in' for the sake of filling in, an experimental

Laure Pigeon Drawing 1938
Collection de l'Art Brut, Paris, courtesy Jean Dubuffet

territory from which she was in due course to elicit recognizable forms. After a while the drawings become airy and light, with a minimum of filling-in; narrow bands like thin bead necklaces are arranged within the four sides of the sheet of paper. Laure's pictorial language, with its febrile strokes and volutes, is one of great finesse and inventiveness. In some drawings a network of interlacing curls and fronds again begins to cover over the ground, producing a fascinating imaginary labyrinth of stalks and tendrils. After about 1936 Laure's minute doodling starts to articulate words, as bit by bit thin strips of writing emerge. A number of words recur frequently in these mediumistic texts: her own name Laure; that of her dead mother Alida; those of André and Annette (her brother and sister in some previous existence), of Pierre (Saint Peter, who had been her husband in a former life) and Denis (her spirit guide); and of Edmond, her real husband, which returns obsessively until 1952. The word *janvier* (January) recurs often enough to suggest a special significance for Laure. Apart from these individual words, the texts are curious amalgams of misspelt words (in normal circumstances Laure wrote perfectly correctly) pressed into visual patterns that tend to make them indecipherable as verbal expression. What can be unravelled gives an impression of generally pointless babbling in which there float references to her sacred mission, momentous events, sacrifices and divine secrets—in short, the tone is that of rather tedious spiritualist writing. It would seem that Laure in fact had no contact with organized spiritualist circles, and that her reading in this area was rudimentary; but if her work is of minor interest as mediumistic revelation, it has its intrinsic value as untutored creation.

In 1945 Laure moved to a flat in the Paris suburbs, and resumed drawing. Verbal elements now fade away as the drawings are taken over by tall and stately female figures draped in diaphanous robes, usually facing to the left and forming a phantom cortège. In 1952, Lily, the sister of Edmond, whose second wife had since died, managed to bring the couple together again. But the relationship was impossible, and was in any case definitively severed by Edmond's sudden death in 1953. Alone once more, Laure entered upon her last phase of creativity, in which she produced about two hundred large drawings in royal blue ink on high quality paper. Using a fine-tipped fountain pen, and displaying great technical control (the rare smudges and blots are adroitly integrated into the design) she traces firm lines again and again across the paper, building up areas of blue which resemble clusters of feathers or leaves. These masses stand out boldly against the white of the surrounding paper; empty gaps within the agglomeration are often given a minimal adjustment so as to hint at the female profile. The names of Lili and Pierre reappear, the capital P of the latter being occasionally

Laure Pigeon Drawing 1947–8
Collection de l'Art Brut, Paris, courtesy Jean Dubuffet

so large that it takes over almost the whole sheet. These last creations of
Laure's are particularly moving. Dubuffet speaks of her triumphant deployment of blue inks in terms of a celebration of death: 'Death, for Laure,
is blue'. Whether or not Laure intended her work to be a literal reflection
of a spirit world beyond normal experience, her inventions can certainly
be said to represent forms deliberately dissociated from the vicissitudes of
her actual life. Rather than classify her work as near-abstract art or as a
mode of sublimation, it is important to acknowledge it as an impressive
record of a fertile creative process that defies definition in aesthetico-
cultural terms.

Laure was by no means unbalanced, being a cheerful and agreeable
person much respected by her neighbours. For thirty years she kept her
drawings hidden from the eyes of all but Lily. When she died in 1965, at
the age of eighty-three, she had amassed some five hundred items, the last
being dated 1964. To leaf through this incredible mass of intricate compositions, each with its date carefully annotated, is a vertiginous experience
that cannot be adequately conveyed through the reproduction of a few
chosen pieces.

See also illustrations page 131.

August Neter 1868–?

Where *art culturel* communicates via a syntax that is normally accessible to all cultivated people, art brut is often abstruse and tends to appeal to levels of response that are not normally on the alert. When artistic expression retreats further and further from normal exchange, in the direction of complete refusal to communicate, it can take on a dangerous attraction for those who have a taste for things unfamiliar. Such attraction has been analysed by Roger Caillois in his book on the fantastic in art. One important category he mentions is the one where the artist is familiar with a system of ideas that the recipient finds totally obscure. 'Fantastic art' of this type can originate in cultures we know nothing about, or be the work of artists who, though in fact they share the same background as ourselves, deliberately cultivate obscurity. Neither alternative in fact qualifies under Caillois' rigorous stipulations for the fantastic; but he does not mention a third possibility, the psychotic artist who, while he may once have had a share in the cultural patterns of the collectivity, and whilst he may not be intentionally obscure (though Dubuffet considers it wrong to speak of purely involuntary effects when considering the art of the mad), nonetheless formulates nigh indecipherable messages that amaze and astound. As Francis Reitmann says of the schizophrenic, 'he has no message about the real world, directed to its inhabitants; he is trying to express an altered world'. Thus what A. Noyes terms his 'self-meaningful communication' may not be communication at all, especially if received by people whose world picture is very alien to the one invented by the madman. The case of August Neter may serve to illustrate this problem.

Neter was born in 1868, the youngest of nine children. After a successful school career, he followed technical courses and became an electrical engineer, travelling in Europe and America. In 1897 he set up his own firm in a German town, and got married. His wife was highly strung; Neter frequented prostitutes, and apparently had sexual problems. He was energetic, though he tended to lose interest in anything that did not directly appeal to him. It was in 1907 that a typical schizophrenic deflection began to assert itself: Neter lost the inclination to work, and his thoughts started to wander. He was in need of a rest, having spent sleepless nights worrying about various inventions and patents of his. But his condition got worse: he had depressions and anxiety feelings, and was hypochondriac. After a suicide attempt, Neter was taken to a mental institution, where he was found to be in the acute phase of a schizophrenic process, involving pronounced sensory disorders. One particular hallucination constituted the primary experience in his new version of reality. One day Neter had seen a vision in the sky of a white screen or stage across which passed a torrent of images—of God, of the Witch who created the world, war scenes,

August Neter *Earth's
axis and hare*
Prinzhorn collection,
Heidelberg

monuments, castles—images flitting past at the rate of ten thousand in half
an hour. Neter interpreted these cinematic revelations as a call to finish
the task of redemption that Christ had left incomplete. The grandiose
delusional system that Neter now developed is one of paranoiac coherence
and exactitude. He saw himself as Christ's representative, a prince and a
king, basing these claims on a complex genealogy that showed his grandmother to have been an illegitimate daughter of Napoleon. Neter himself
became 'Août—IV—Napoleon', translating his own first name as the name
of the month. A pretender to several thrones and emperor of France and
Germany, he established a global hierarchy in which his was the highest
authority, he being the new Redeemer designated by God, and Napoleon's
heir. The tyranny of his imagination was such that he could take all women
to be his own; even the nuns who worked in the institution were seen as
concubines of his in disguise! (Despite his erotic fantasies about them, he
in fact treated them with the utmost respect.) Outwardly Neter still showed
some of the self-confident manners of the man of the world, though in
truth he had become autistic to an extreme. He upheld two concurrent
identities, being both engineer-patient and emperor-redeemer; but he
was careful not to mix them, and laid far more weight on the latter identity,
obviously more 'real' to him than the world of appearances of the hospital.
Though there are traces of a tension between his status as inmate and
that as all-mighty emperor, it may be concluded that the power of his
imagination was greater than that of objective fact.

Neter began in 1911 to produce a number of fascinating drawings,
executed with fanatic precision with a sharp pencil and a ruler, some
designs often being patiently repeated with slight variants before a final
version was perfected. These drawings, reminiscent of technical diagrams,
are in fact copies of the images imprinted by the great hallucination.
Prinzhorn sounds a warning not to overlook the likelihood of subsequent
elaboration upon the original vision, as well as playful additions at the

August Neter *Antichrist*
Prinzhorn collection, Heidelberg

August Neter *The miraculous shepherd*
Prinzhorn collection, Heidelberg

stage of composition. However the lengthy descriptions given by Neter seem authoritative enough.

The picture entitled *Antichrist* is a precisely drawn, austere image of a figure with outstretched arms emanating from a cloud or a face in profile. According to Neter, this is 'St Thomas, God's spirit in the figure of the false prophet standing on a cloud and proclaiming to the Redeemer the last judgement that condemns sinful mankind.' Neter tells us that the name Thomas stands for Disbelief, and that the figure is in the shape of a T made up of three commas (thus: T(c)ommas, a punning association). The prophet's head is composed of an artillery shell which changes into a papal tiara, and finally a bundle of straw. The drawing *Earth's axis and hare* records another of the ten thousand images, and depicts a log on its side. This is Neter's genealogical tree. It is equipped with rings to denote the years of growth, as well as horse's or goat's hooves (the Devil) at one extremity and God's hands laid at the other. A hare jumps out of a cloud on to the cylinder, which begins to revolve. This hare symbolizes 'the fragility

96

of happiness', and the picture as a whole is an allusion to war—the outline of a glass in the top right hand corner denotes the hare's cup of suffering. The drawing of *The miraculous shepherd* is a yet more complex concentration, forming a kind of personal totem replete with associations and symbols. Neter's exegesis speaks of an erect cobra, a leg running beside it, a second leg formed out of a root, the face of his father-in-law, a tree whose branches take the form of hair, the female sexual organ (placed so as to break off the man's foot and thus symbolize the Fall), and the Good Shepherd, Neter himself, who is surrounded by wolves in sheep's clothing (the shepherd's garment is marked with the letter w, which is the initial of the words 'wolf' and 'wool', and in German is pronounced like the word *Weh*, which means suffering). The sheer sexuality of the picture seems to be belied by the innocent expression on the shepherd's face.

The taut economy of these pictorial compressions and suggestions is only completely brought out by the commentaries, which are, one might argue, integral to the drawings. Prinzhorn writes that Neter's images seize us as being representations of the schizophrenic experience in all its nakedness: such pictures cannot possibly be amenable to a rational or an aesthetic approach. What one should do is try to plot exactly what makes these drawings *unheimlich*, disturbing or fantastic: to guess at the process whereby the psychotic screw is subtly turned to transmute the familiar into the strange, and thence into the inaccessible. Can we find something attractive in images such as these, whose mechanisms resist our 'normal' understanding? If we are attracted, we shall probably be stimulated to undertake some sort of enquiry into Neter's delusional system. What outcome should we then anticipate? Would not a full understanding of Neter's autistic world tend to make the unfamiliar so clear that his images would come out as flat and uninteresting? The answer is likely to be no—for once one was intimate with Neter's way of thinking one would probably share his unfailing delight in the exclusivity of 'self-meaningful communication'; one would be *on the inside*, where the external criteria of aesthetic form and adequate technique are no longer operative.

See also illustration page 28.

Gaston Duf 1920–

Gaston Duf was born in 1920 in the mining area of the Pas-de-Calais. His parents were not married. His father kept a café, and was a drunkard who terrorized his children. Timid and retiring, Gaston always turned for protection to his mother. At fourteen he left school and worked as a baker's apprentice and then as a surface worker at the mines. He was unreliable, and was often off sick. When he was eighteen his parents finally married. Gaston reacted wildly, getting drunk and making scenes, then lapsing into apathy. In 1940, after a suicide attempt, he was committed to an asylum in Lille where he declared that his parents had been trying to poison him. His behaviour was generally calm, but there were outbursts of violence, including a further attempted suicide. He spent much of his time before a mirror carefully combing his hair, with three impeccable partings. After a while, it was noticed that he was doing drawings on bits of paper and stuffing them in his pockets. This creative work was encouraged when, with unusual perception, his doctor made available to him exercise books and then water-colours, which Gaston learned to apply with surprising skill. He explained that his work was encouraged by Pâpâ Mins'oüzzss, a police inspector with a black moustache who was his 'true' father. Gaston also spoke of a second putative father, Pâpâ Lôé, or God; both versions were later synthesized into the one protective figure.

Gaston's obsessive subject is a monstrous rhinoceros, a creature with huge eyes, horn and squat legs with great vegetal excrescences. Gaston said he had once seen a rhinoceros in a film about the jungle; but it is of little relevance to establish to what degree his rhinoceros is compatible with our idea of that animal. What is important is the symbolic and emotional significance it had for Gaston. He himself stated that the massive beast meant a lot to him because it was hard and strong, the exact opposite of the soft weakling that he was. The medical interpretation would be to see the rhinoceros as a virility symbol, an imaginary rival to Gaston's hated father. Yet Gaston's insistence on drawing the animal again and again, constantly altering the details, indicates that this is only part of the story. The rhinoceros became the pretext for an infinite sequence of variations, a neomorphism (invented form) that could render for him as many meanings as he wanted. In this sense, as Dubuffet points out, Gaston's rhinoceros is indeterminate and polyvalent: it is a heraldic, abstracted creature, less meaningful *per se* than the variations which it encourages. From time to time Gaston drew other animals: hippopotami (very similar to the rhino-ceroses), crocodiles, tortoises, cows, etc. He also drew birds: parrots, pigeons, pheasants, etc., again making the initial subject into something fantastic or aberrant. There are, finally, drawings of clown-like human figures and a number of objects: guns, flower-pots, spoons.

Gaston Duf *Crôqôdille Ippôtâme* about 1948
Collection de l'Art Brut, Paris, courtesy Jean Dubuffet

As rebarbative as the drawings are the titles and inscriptions that adorn them, and in which Gaston's passion for variations gives rise to a galaxy of alternative spellings. His variations on the word *rhinocéros* are the result of an engrossing spelling-game: *rinâûçêrshôse, rônâûsêrôse, rin'-hâûçêr'-hâûs'-he, lin-'hôçêr-'hâûshe*—these are but a few of Gaston's neologisms, in which bristling cedillas and circumflex accents together with the shifting letters create a truly outlandish orthography. Gaston obviously gave a lot of thought to these deformations, for no two are the same. In so doing, he must have lost from view the notion 'rhinoceros = jungle animal', and have developed the concept in a purely abstract way. Gaston's private zoology, backed by this private language, thus constitutes a sustained violation of accepted representations of external things and a celebration of independent creation.

After 1953, Gaston abandoned his drawings, and grew fat and listless. When his doctor persuaded him to draw again, he did a few rhinoceroses, but had lost his enthusiasm and skill. It seems that the abstracted image had turned back into something figurative: Gaston now declared that he was afraid of those 'monsters', which now seemed to symbolize guilty sexual feelings. The emblem of inspired abstraction had hardened into a malefic object. Thereafter, having for a while projected his autistic thoughts in a form that was to some degree intelligible to others (and it is in the sense that it is *still* accessible whilst *tending* to be inaccessible that Gaston's work qualifies as art brut), he moved to the extreme autistic position, retreating to a point of catatonic indifference such that it became impossible to establish any further contact with him, or to assess whether anything was going on at all behind the closed doors of his autistic theatre.

Opposite, above
Gaston Duf *Rinâûsêrôse Vilritiès* about 1948
Collection de l'Art Brut, Paris, courtesy Jean Dubuffet

Opposite, below
Gaston Duf *Une Pintâde Blenêthe* about 1948
Collection de l'Art Brut, Paris, courtesy Jean Dubuffet
See also illustration page 125.

Augustin Lesage 1876–1954

I was at work, lying down in a narrow trench opening out onto a
gallery well away from the main workings of the mine. In the silence,
all I could hear was the noise of my pick. When all of a sudden I heard
a voice, a very clear voice, that said: 'One day you will be a painter!'
I looked all round to see where the voice was coming from. There was
nobody there. I was quite alone. I was amazed and scared. When I
came up from the mine, I spoke about this to no-one, neither my
friends, my children, nor my wife. I was afraid that I would be taken
for a crank or a madman.

These were the terms in which Augustin Lesage described his first supernatural experience. At the time of speaking, Lesage had become an established medium and painter, and had been invited to Paris to give a
public demonstration at the Institut métapsychique. His remarks, recorded
during an interview with Dr Eugène Osty, are characterized by a naïve
wonder at the circumstances of his mediumship. Some might see his account
as the invention of a cunning mind, others as the elaboration of a gullible
fool. While it seems unlikely that Lesage made up the whole story, it is
not plausible to suppose that he was totally innocent of the effect it had
on others—which is to suggest a certain amount of playing-up to the role
that the Paris specialists were eager to applaud. However, rather than
speculate on Lesage's authenticity as a medium, it is more important to
summarize his story as prelude to a consideration of his actual paintings
and their validity as *créations d'art*.

Lesage was born in 1876 at Auchel in the Pas-de-Calais, the most important mining region in France. After attending primary school, where
he received without enthusiasm the minimal instruction in how to draw
that every child was given, at the age of fourteen he became a miner.
During his military service, he happened to go into a public gallery in Lille,
but showed no interest at all in the pictures. In 1900 he was back at work,
living in Burbure, where he married and had a family. Lesage was an un-
exceptional working man who had not the slightest cultural pretentions.
But one day in 1911 he heard a voice telling him he would be a painter,
and later came to conclude that this had been a message from a spirit.
Spiritualist ideas had a firm hold on the people of the Pas-de-Calais, and
Lesage soon found friends willing to try to make contact with the supernatural realm. After a number of séances, Lesage began to draw under
the control of spirit guides, who insisted that he buy some paints. The
miner made for the local art shop and managed to acquire the necessary
materials, despite his embarrassed ignorance; the spirits, it appears,
guided his hands in choosing the tubes of colour. A friend ordered a canvas

for him; when it arrived it turned out to be three metres square! But encouraged by his spirits, Lesage set it up in his front room, in full view of the neighbours, and began painting. Starting in the top right hand corner, he gradually worked his way down across the vast area, adding detail upon detail to complete a painting of astonishing size and complexity. The composition unites hundreds of little subjects, human figures, architectural motifs and stylized vegetation, each of which is a painting in its own right. It is as though Lesage was impatient to try out an inexhaustible supply of inspirations. The brilliant fits and starts are piled up into a fantastic pictorial structure so immense that it defies any global analysis. Crammed as it is with apparent reminiscences of Egyptian and Oriental art, and executed with a finesse worthy of an Old Master, it is hard to believe that this unique painting is the work of an uneducated workman who had previously spent twenty years of his life wielding a pick at the coal-face.*

In 1914 Lesage was brought before a tribunal after complaints by the local doctor's union. With a friend versed in 'magnetism', he had been practising spiritualist healing, as a kind of supplement to his artistic inspiration. The testimony of thirty of his satisfied patients was sufficient to acquit him fully. Later that year he was called up to the front, where he spent his free time drawing in coloured pencils, obviously pleased that everyone took him to be a professional artist. By the end of the war he had returned to the mine and to his painting. By 1923 he had attracted such attention from spiritualist circles that he resolved to retire and devote all his time to his art. By 1925 he was having pictures exhibited at the Spiritualist Congress in Paris and even in proper art galleries. His examination in 1927 by Dr Osty, the president of the Institut métapsychique, was the final confirmation of his position as a recognized medium and painter. At his death in 1954 he had completed an estimated eight hundred canvases.

In the works that follow his first and finest painting, Lesage developed a rigorous technique. He would begin a picture by tracing a precise median line down the centre of the canvas, and then work his way down from the top. Details placed on one side of the line would reappear on the other to create a perfectly symmetrical design. Sometimes he left unpainted gaps, which are also precisely balanced on either side of the vertical axis. According to Osty's observations, Lesage did not need to look across the

---

* Lesage's masterpiece is now in the Collection de l'Art Brut in Paris. It is reproduced, in full and with details, in *L'Art Brut* no. 3, together with Osty's report (see below). In his report, Dr Osty quotes certificates supplied by the local mayor and the director of the mine which declare Lesage's complete lack of artistic training.

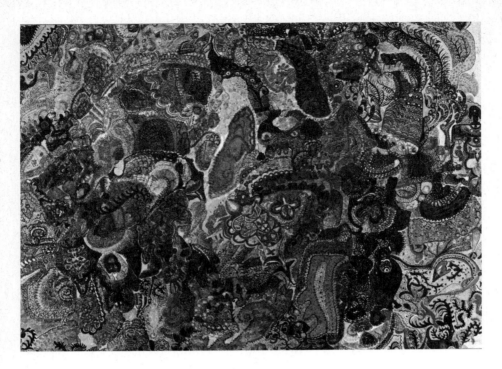

Augustin Lesage Detail from top right-hand corner of his first painting 1912–13
Collection de l'Art Brut, Paris, courtesy Jean Dubuffet

wide distance between two corresponding points: the brushstroke mirroring
what was on the far side of the canvas was executed with faultless precision,
without his having to check. Lesage scarcely ever faltered; and when he
did make one of his rare mistakes, he would, so he claims, feel an immediate
unease that made him step back from the canvas and spot the inconsistency.
Never did he have any idea of what he was going to paint before he started.
His guides controlled every change of colour, every least stroke of the
brush. 'Do not try to find out what you are doing', they told him. Accordingly,
Lesage had only to attend to their dictation, abandoning himself to an
ecstatic state in which everything would seem to vibrate about him, with
delightful bells ringing in his ears for as long as he was not interrupted.

The art of Lesage is vaguely reminiscent of other styles that one feels
one knows. Yet of which, exactly? Osty found it impossible to pin down
any specific resemblances, even after combing through all the art styles of
Tibet, Mexico, Indochina, India and Egypt. At the Louvre, he scanned
the mosaics, columns, vases and sarcophagi of ancient civilizations, yet
found no defensible analogy between any one detail of these and Lesage's
work.

Admittedly Lesage, responding to the fashionable spiritualist interest in
anything reminiscent of Ancient Egypt, did use some details of apparently
Egyptian character, such as hieroglyphs. However this happened only at
a later stage, at a time when public attention to his work had begun to
draw Lesage across the line that separates autonomous creation from
creation that, being orientated towards an audience, loses its self-absorbed

intensity, and becomes facile and ingratiating. Lesage's later works purport to be 'masterpieces' in the worst sense: they are conscious advertisements of the painter's virtuosity. Decoration has become coy and would-be enticing, and lacks the 'primitive' richness of the earlier idiosyncratic vision. The 'ornamental' has taken over from the 'mental'; that is, the idiom that truly articulates Lesage's mind has been deformed by a cajoling ego which stipulates that dazzling performance is better than anguished truth. When the sign no longer *lives*, it becomes a dead letter, losing its plural dimension and dwindling into redundant cliché.

The use of signatures by Lesage reflects this deterioration in expressivity. The first painting was unsigned. Subsequent work up to 1925 was signed 'Léonard de Vinci'. It was very likely the famous theft of the Mona Lisa in 1911 that brought this name to Lesage's attention. That he adopted it, meant that he needed an alibi. To tell his friends that his work emanated from a spirit world, being dictated by a famous painter from the past, meant that he could avoid responsibility and therefore ridicule. After it had dawned on him that Da Vinci's actual style while alive was rather different from the style he was now supposedly transmitting from the next world, Lesage began to use a different pseudonym, Marius de Tyane. The name of this painter, allegedly a great artist of ancient times, is unknown to historians (though it has been suggested that Lesage was thinking of Apollonius de Tyane, a thaumaturge of the first century AD, who was not in fact a painter). It appears that after reading about the doctrine of reincarnation as expounded by Allen Kardec and his disciples, Lesage had revised his ideas, and now fancied himself as the *reincarnation* of a great painter from the past. Though uncertain whether to think of himself as a Hindu or an Egyptian artist, Lesage ignored the contradictions in his explanation, and felt secure in the new identity he had chosen. In effect he had moved from the status of mere medium to that of actual creator; for a while he signed 'Médium Lesage', and finally 'Augustin Lesage'. It may be noted that his 'medium' story had by now been more or less disproven (Osty's test of asking him to paint in total darkness had led to a lamentable failure), and one may deduce that the switch to the more self-centred explanation of his inspiration was motivated by vanity. He was now fully 'responsible': no longer an intermediary, an apprentice, he was Lesage the Artist. My argument is that the naïveté of these revisions is paralleled by the naïveté of the later work, which is coy, empty and altogether inferior to the early pictures, whose uninfluenced primitivism remains wholly admirable.

See also illustration page 45.

Jules Dou 1884–1946

Born in the Swiss canton of Vaud in 1884, and one of a family of ten children, Jules had an alcoholic father who hanged himself when Jules was eleven. One of his brothers also ended up an alcoholic. Jules left school in his early teens, having acquired little culture and no artistic training. He drifted from job to job, finally settling as pointsman on the railways. After a broken engagement, he began to drink and to develop a persecution mania, imagining that people were pointing at him and talking about him. Seeking isolation, he took a job as servant in the country, but still felt pursued: he claimed later that his unusually fine hearing enabled him to pick up the things that people were whispering behind his back. On top of this he felt an emptiness in his chest that hindered his breathing, and could hear his heart beating loudly. In 1910, at the age of twenty-six, he was interned in a clinic after having attacked his mother with a stick. He was a highly re-calcitrant patient, running away on two occasions and otherwise behaving violently in a way that was extremely difficult to control. For some fifteen years he remained in this agitated and aggressive state, persistently scratching himself till he drew blood. In 1927, now forty-three, Jules suddenly began to draw for the first time, producing in the space of a few months hundreds of pencil drawings on small pieces of wrapping paper. He continued very intermittently for ten years after this initial period, and then ceased all further production. He died in 1946.

The spontaneous outburst of Jules' creativity is no less remarkable than the originality of his style, endorsed as it is by total lack of training or academic orientation. His themes are simple enough: scenes of country life, domestic animals, fishermen, footballers, wrestlers. What is impressive is the surety of his lines, the unhesitating rhythms of his curves and spirals. The deformations he carries out on his figures are, like the studied mis-spellings of his titles, the result of an abnormative and yet highly animated process of schizophrenic reconstruction. Jules bends his lines to produce impossible distortions of the human body; one man will lose an arm, another will grow a hand from his buttocks. In a set of drawings grouped here under the title *William Tell*, one can witness the stages of a process of agglutination of two forms, and the final absorption of one by the other. The paternal hand, placed protectively on the son's head, appears gradually to pull the head inside the father, in a disturbingly ambivalent image that suggests both protectiveness and ogrish devouring. (The last drawing in

Jules Dou *William Tell*
Reproduced from *Though this be madness* (*Insania pingens*) by A. Bader, H. Steck, G. Schmidt, J. Cocteau (Thames and Hudson, London, 1961) by kind permission of Dr Alfred Bader

Jules Dou *Monzieur rentrant à lat Maizon out à Butdatpest* (*Gentleman returning home or in Budapest*)
Collection de l'Art Brut, Paris, courtesy Jean Dubuffet

the set apparently shows an arrow hitting an apple or an eye, possibly a visual pun in the sense that Tell's son is 'the apple of his eye'.) The singularity of Jules' warped shapes is curiously enhanced by the way he fills them in, though in fact he draws on a very limited range of stereotype patterns: shading, hatching, stippling, and use of squares, circles and repeated letters.

The Abbé Fouéré 1842–1910

Abbé Fouéré *Rock sculptures at Rothéneuf*
Reproduced by kind permission of H. Brebion

At Rothéneuf, east of Saint-Malo on the Brittany coast, there flourished
from the mid-sixteenth century until the Revolution a corsair clan
notorious for its brutal rapacity and savage pride. Equipped with light,
fast ships, the band of smugglers, fishermen and pirates was able to rival
the great fleets of Saint-Malo itself, and held sway over an area extending
out to the Channel Islands. Over the centuries, as accounts of their intrepid
exploits blended into legend, so their names were given to rocks and reefs
all along the coast. The clan finally perished as a result of fratricidal battles
at the time of the Revolution, culminating in a pitched sea-fight in which
the last of the Rothéneuf were wiped out: the legend has it that a great
storm destroyed the vanquished ships and tossed the dead and dying into

the sea to be swallowed up by hideous monsters of the deep, in truly apocalyptic fashion.

It was on a small promontory between two deep creeks sticking out from the shore at Rothéneuf, where once the pirates had prayed before the rough altar of the mariners' patron Saint Budoc, that towards the end of the last century an obscure hermit decided to carve a complex of sculptures into the rock, turning part of the actual site of their exploits into a monument to the Rothéneuf pirates. The great mass of granite was gouged and broken to form the writhing limbs and gaunt faces of those giants of the sea: Jacques de Limoelou, the solitary lookout; Le Guemereux, called the 'fakir' and renowned for his predictions; the fearful chieftains known as Gargantua and Lucifer; Jean de Caulnes, the 'Egyptian', who courted his leader's wife; and the last of the corsairs, Monsieur de Rothéneuf himself. The figures loom proudly up like seamarks, or float in anguished masses amid ferocious beasts. The massive piece of sculpted rock lies open to the wind and rain, and is even periodically attacked by the tides.

The hermit who carved out this barbaric epic was Adolphe-Julien Fouéré, born an illegitimate child in 1842. Nothing is known of his ecclesiastical career, save that the local population referred to him as the onetime rector. Possibly he quarrelled with his superiors before retiring to his house on the cliffs, which he named 'Haute Folie'. It seems likely that the altar to Saint Budoc carved into the rock in the seventeenth century inspired his mammoth task. Fouéré began at the age of forty-three, and worked for twenty-five years or more, with the sole assistance of a simple old man. The achievement is remarkable. The sculptures arose out of the rock formations which suggested shapes for Fouéré to carve out, the cramped deformations of his style being thus the fruit of a collaboration of Nature and an imagination possessed by visions of grandeur and catastrophe. In their blind, unsophisticated roughness, the Rochers Sculptés at Rothéneuf are a noteworthy example of raw creation.

Gilbert 1915–

As a child in South-East London, Gilbert used to watch the trains pass by at the bottom of the garden, and played at being a railway-engine. During the war he was nursed by an aunt and developed a fixation for the hollow of her neck, which became the stimulus for subsequent sexual fantasies. A timorous and backward boy, he made no friends and hated school, being incapable of completing the work set and often incurring his teachers' wrath by involuntary catcalls. Despite his apparently low intelligence, the drawings and texts that Gilbert produced during treatment for schizophrenia in a London hospital in 1937 are evidence of a meticulous mind. The drawings themselves are unoriginal, and are undoubtedly based on book illustrations. The bias is to architectural motifs: pyramids, Gothic crosses, Tudor chimneys, church towers and factory buildings with large smokestacks. These drawings are arranged by Gilbert according to their greater or lesser complexity: he had established a kind of catalogue of shapes in which, grouped according to what he calls 'themes' (basic shapes) such as chimneys, cowls, funnels, vases, etc., are listed the variants on each design, the apparent intention being to implement these into a range of permutations. Furthermore, to each basic shape is attached a group of neologisms, usually without any logical connexion with the object depicted and cultivated largely according to clang associations. The drawing *Cordron* (see over) shows the way patterns such as are used in wrought-iron work are built up from a small repertoire of simple motifs, to each of which is attributed a set of words. Here may be detected a preference for particular sounds, as for example the glottal end-syllable on words like 'squirrel' or 'shingle'. The non-applicability of this vocabulary is hard to explain, and the impression it gives is of that meaningless consistency that Prinzhorn defined as *pointenlose Konsequenz*. On the one hand this could be a purely 'abstract' game with nonsense words whose sole function is to declare their inventor's privacy. At the other extreme, they may have complex connotations and constitute a rich and meaningful code. Certainly it was typical of Gilbert's character that he should turn from the harsh external world into the docile world of a personal language. He once remarked: 'When I look at things, the thought of a word comes into my head. The word seems to match it.' This invented word may both fully divert attention from that to which ostensibly it points, and be so highly charged that it takes on an almost concrete reality for its creator. Not enough material is available to permit further speculation on this point; what evidence there is suggests that Gilbert's system was in an early stage of elaboration, being coherent in parts and haphazard in others.

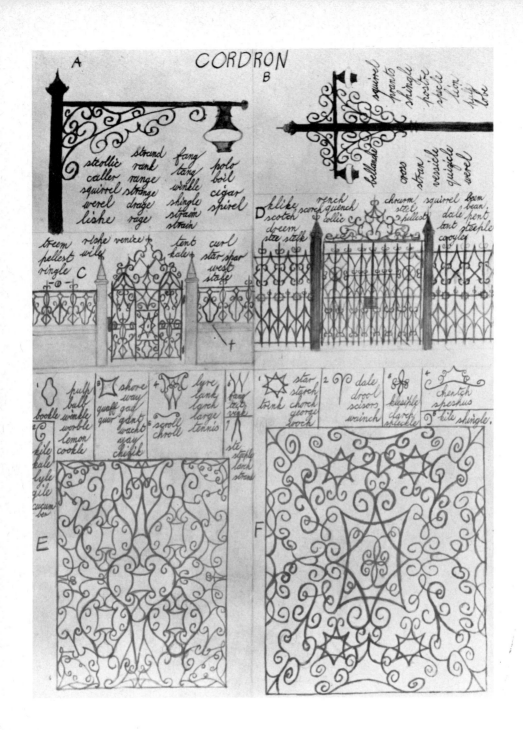

Gilbert *Cordron* 1937
Guttman-Maclay collection, London

Joseph Crépin 1875–1948

The mediumistic artist Joseph Crépin was born in 1875 in Hénin-Liétard in the Pas-de-Calais, not far from Lesage's birthplace. As a child, he had to have two operations on his eyes, and in later life claimed that he could stare directly at the sun several times a week. When he left school at about fourteen, Crépin went into his father's plumbing and roof-mending business. He had musical talent, and played and composed for the clarinet. His music was written out with extreme tidiness and an eye for its visual effect. Later on, Crépin directed a miners' brass band, which often performed his compositions, and in due course the trumpet society of Hénin-Liétard itself, winning several competition prizes. Much of his leisure time was spent copying out music for his friends. In 1901 he got married, and settled in the nearby village of Montigny-en-Gohelle. He had two daughters, one of whom went mad at the age of twenty-five and had to be kept locked up for years at the back of the house. Crépin now had his own business: his wife ran an ironmongery shop while he and three employees worked mainly at drilling wells and installing pumps. In 1930 Crépin met Victor Simon, a friend and follower of Lesage, and himself a medium and painter. Through him Crépin met Lesage, and later joined the Spiritualist Circle at Arras. Yet for the time being his spiritualist interests were not pictorial. Already, as a result of his work, he had become aware of his 'radiesthetic' powers as a water-diviner, using a watch swinging at the end of its chain. Now he found that through the same pendulum he could detect and cure diseases, and soon acquired a reputation as a healer who worked through the laying-on of hands, and even carried out cures telepathically. In time Crépin became practically a professional healer, and, as Lesage had done, withstood attacks launched by the medical union by displaying sheaves of glowing testimonials.

It was in 1938, when Crépin was sixty-three years old, that one evening, while he was copying out some music, his hand ceased to obey him and began to draw intriguing little designs on the paper. Encouraged by his friends, Crépin began filling exercise books with scores of motifs. Later, he copied these out on large sheets, using coloured pencils, and by 1939 had moved on to proper oil painting, producing a regular supply of pictures. He had a great sense of economy, and never wasted a thing, conscientiously ticking off each motif in his design book as he painted it up, and meticulously numbering each finished item. The paintings suggest temples or heraldic statues, and have a pronounced tendency to abstraction, although one can make out some figurines and stylized birds and snakes. But the dominant characteristic of Crépin's work is its almost fanatical attention to symmetry, which, as has been seen, was the key element in Lesage's work. Crépin's first drawings were done on cross-ruled paper, which clearly encouraged

Joseph Crépin Painting no. 82, 1940
Collection Micheline and Vincent Bounoure, Paris

Opposite
Joseph Crépin Painting no. 32, 1939
Collection de l'Art Brut, Paris, courtesy Jean Dubuffet

him to elaborate balanced designs, the little square being the basic unit
in a structure that could be exactly bisected by a vertical line running
down its centre. Dubuffet suggests that Crépin's art is fundamentally
anti-natural, for nature very rarely produces anything so mathematically
symmetrical. (When one does come across specimens such as perfect
crystals, they may strike one as rather uncanny aberrations.) In this sense,
Crépin's paintings are highly cerebral, and may elicit an intuition of
something higher than the natural order, namely the supernatural. As
Dubuffet puts it, 'symmetry is the implacable constraint, it is Order, it is
the end of being'. The rigorously deterministic pictorial scheme has the

austere solemnity of some unspeakable ritual that stifles all freedom and caprice. When faced with such pictures, the eyes flicker nervously in a pendular motion from side to side to check that everything is in its place; the occasional intrusion of three-dimensional perspectives into the overall two-dimensional plane, adds to the sense of disturbance. The inexorable pulsation of the patterns may even have an hypnotic effect, and seem to close in on the onlooker.

After his wife's death in 1943, Crépin's mad daughter was put in an institution, and he lived alone with his other daughter, Benoîte. During the war, he would paint by night, listening to concerts on the radio or to his daughter playing the violin in the next room; no one actually watched him at work. It was now that he heard a voice telling him that when he had completed three hundred paintings, the war would be over. Sure enough, his three-hundredth picture was signed on 7 May 1945. The voice had also told him that he would go on to do forty-five *tableaux merveilleux*, after which the whole world would be at peace. Crépin died in 1948, having completed only forty-three of this series. 'Marvellous pictures' were the name he gave to works carried out according to a new technique he had discovered for applying tiny luminous globules of paint, apparently mixed with varnish, and which studded the surface like brightly-coloured beads. Crépin was very proud of this invention, and claimed to be able to apply fifteen hundred of them in an hour, without glasses. It is thought that he must have used a tool like a baker's icing-pump in order to place the drops of paint with such accuracy. Certainly Crépin attained an inhuman precision, his paintings becoming more and more like glistening machines, so perfect that they seem not to be subject to the laws of nature. Like inhumanly rigid musical scores in appearance, these images no longer function as art, but become magical talismans. Their miraculous powers were such that the dwellings of all those people who owned Crépin pictures were spared during the heavy wartime bombardments that ravaged the whole region.

See also illustration page 128.

Palanc 1928–

Palanc is a pastry-cook. Born Francis Palanque in Vence, he left school at sixteen to learn his trade from his parents, showing a marked aptitude for designs in icing-sugar. He has a somewhat moody temperament, and under the stress of disagreements within the family circle, he turned to private meditations of a metaphysical nature. At about the age of nineteen he began to experiment with an alphabet of invented letters, a system of highly angular signs (possibly, he once hinted, as the result of seeing Egyptian or Chinese characters). This *écriturisme*, as he calls it, is something that he can never feel he has perfected, for over the years he has not ceased to adapt and renew it, often destroying outmoded material. He has an appetite for precise organization and, one feels, a taste for complexity for its own sake. Early on, he discovered that his researches could only proceed if he thought in terms of two parallel alphabets, one with 'closed' characters, the other with 'open' ones. When he writes, these letters join together to form zigzag lines that run diagonally down the page. A private code, this writing has also a visual appeal, formulated by Dubuffet as its 'skeletal poetry'.

When he feels tense, Palanc carries out exercises in front of a blackboard which he has set up in his bedroom, and upon which, with chalk in either hand, he traces circles or squares using expansive movements of the arms. From this practice he derives release from tension and often mental stimulation for his researches. He has drawn up a treatise, *L'Autogéométrie*, to explain the psycho-physical benefits of this form of geometrical gymnastics. The treatise contains a number of illustrations in which a manikin (representing either a man or a woman according to whether it is entirely angular or is in part made up of curves) stands before a blackboard and draws lines upon it. Straight lines ('ruler gesture') and curves ('compass gesture') are the two basic types of line; it is through a gradual mastery of their execution, achieved in conjunction with breathing exercises, that the practitioner can attain a psycho-physical equilibrium. According to Palanc, these exercises stimulate the unconscious to fertilize the conscious mind, in turn influencing the physical being. The discipline can also have positive effects in terms of social adaptation.

These theories are implemented in Palanc's pictures, which are composed with the same care that he devotes to his pastries, and indeed reflect some of the techniques of his trade. He usually starts by spreading gum on to a panel, and then applies more or less fine preparations of crushed egg-shells (or, occasionally, sawdust), dyed in different colours, sprinkling them over the appropriate areas of the picture by means of a sifter. The picture plane is crossed by lines that spell out phrases in one of his alphabets, together with other geometrical patterns. As the lines cross each other and delineate

separate areas, these are given distinct colours so that the writing stands out clearly as a silhouette of jagged angles. Sometimes Palanc transcribes the text in normal French on the back of the picture. All in all, his paintings demonstrate a close interconnection of words and visual forms, the new alphabet being so to speak at once text and plastic shape. 'All is words. Everything that is a word is more or less a form', writes Palanc. 'Everything

that is a form more or less penetrates itself, is more or less penetrated, more
or less envelops itself, is more or less enveloped.' His premise seems to be
that verbal language is a structure of interlocking parts, a geometrical
diagram which, if one can master its complexities, can put one in tune with
universal truth.

The latent erotic content of these elucubrations—the balancing of male
and female forms: lines and circles, open and closed letters—together with
the notion of a spiritual discipline is reminiscent of certain aspects of Oriental
metaphysics. Certainly Palanc is more concerned with the innate virtue
of his system than with its exploitation; he is not at all interested in the
aesthetic aspect of his work. After being persuaded to exhibit at a local
art gallery in 1959, he found the situation intolerable and reacted by
destroying a whole series of finished pictures with an axe, with the result
that only about a tenth of his works are now extant. Since this act of an-
nihilation, he appears to have abandoned further production.

Peter Moog 1871–?

Peter Moog did well at school, and was good at drawing and woodwork. He made his way in life as a barman, and eventually became a landlord himself, though this venture ended in bankruptcy. He was jolly and easy-going, always ready to joke with his customers, and much given to drinking and womanizing. His marriage was unsuccessful, and his wife died in 1907. While checking his accounts one day in 1908, Moog was suddenly hit by what he called an electric shock in his brain that at once revealed to him that he was a great poet and artist, the equal of Goethe and Schiller. After a few weeks of euphoric wandering around the countryside, he was committed to an asylum. He adjusted at once to his new surroundings, showing a manic buoyancy of mood, joking all the time and showing off about his great riches—once gathering pebbles and bits of glass from the garden to demonstrate unlimited cash in hand. As a millionaire and owner of great estates, he planned all manner of charitable endowments, and drew up projects for an airship to carry 3600 passengers and an art museum to which he would undertake to contribute two to three pictures daily. He wrote ceremonious letters to the director of the asylum, to the crown princess of Greece, and to his imaginary fiancée Amalie, who was sent idealizing love poems signed 'Friedrich von Schiller' in an envelope addressed 'Heavenly Kingdom, 500 Paradise Street, in the angels' sugar-box'. Moog settled down to a busy existence in the asylum, doing odd jobs and even clerical work in the office. He made great show of his ascetic piety, renouncing tobacco and drink, and devoting himself to his higher calling as a religious artist, the creator of holy images. Moog's works are large ink and water-colour pictures of lofty and solemn tone. Around a large central figure are grouped smaller ones, the remaining spaces being filled with steeples or decorative designs. The *Last Judgement* depicts Christ descending to earth with a pair of scales, flanked by angels with trumpets and swords. Above, God holds open the book of reckoning. About a crucifix are gathered those resurrected souls intended for heaven (a ladder is provided). On the right is Heaven itself, a complex of delightfully appointed rooms with balconies that extend up and up. To the left, the damned undergo torture at the hands of devils and demons. At the bottom of the picture little graves are laid out in orderly rows to illustrate the saying that Moog points out in his commentary: when one masturbates one kills an angel. Another composition, the *Destruction of Jerusalem*, stacks up dozens of religious scenes, including one of the Madonna aboard a chariot drawn by seven knights of St George, who are locked in deadly combat with a dragon. Moog assures us that they have special shields to protect their faces against the spouting of its poisonous blood.

Moog's art reflects a struggle to atone for his dissipated life, and

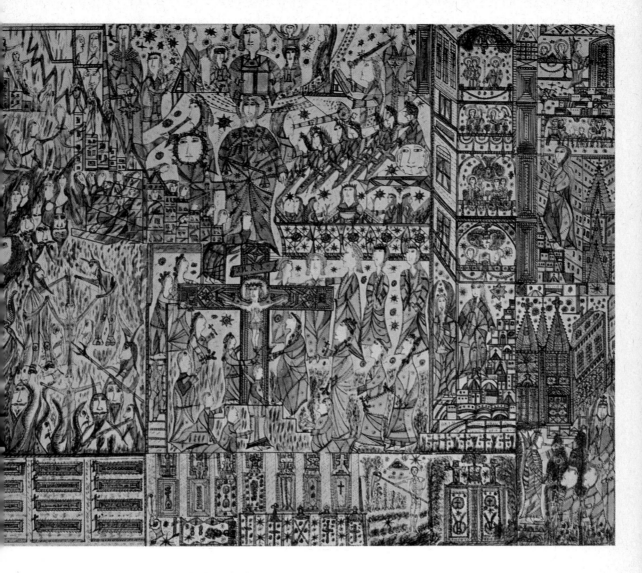

Peter Moog *The Last Judgement*
Prinzhorn collection, Heidelberg

represents a somewhat pathetic sublimation of his instincts. The pious
images, probably reminiscences of his home-town church, have a Byzantine-
like rigidity. A product of guilt feelings, they feel cramped and ingratiating,
and show perhaps too much concern for known models and an audience
to be counted as fully valid examples of art brut—though there is a certain
charm in Moog's insertion of incongruent and comical detail into the
grandiose overall scheme.

Scottie Wilson *Self-portrait with Greedies*
Collection Paul Eluard, Paris

Guillaume *The tiger hunt* 1938
Collection de l'Art Brut,
Paris, courtesy Jean
Dubuffet

Guillaume *The eagles, the goose's feather* 1940
Collection de l'Art Brut,
Paris, courtesy Jean
Dubuffet

Scottie Wilson *Scottie's art gallery no. 2* 1949
Brook Street Gallery, London

Gaston Duf *Pôlichinéllle Rôflise Vilôse* 1956
Collection de l'Art Brut, Paris, courtesy Jean Dubuffet

Gaston Chaissac 1910–64

Astride the borderline that demarcates pure art brut stands Gaston Chaissac,
an innocent aware of his innocence. Born in Avallon in 1910, he worked
for years as a shoemaker in the country, and his paintings and objects
have an authentic rawness that contains no trace of cultural ingredients.
Doubt as to Chaissac's integral detachment from culture arises from the
fact that from 1938 he exhibited regularly in Parisian and provincial galleries,
and corresponded regularly with Paris intellectuals and artists—a selection
of his letters was published by the literary firm of Gallimard in 1951. Yet
for all these contacts, and despite his literary gifts, Chaissac remained a
modest peasant who kept on stepping back outside cultural limits with
remarks such as this: 'I've always preferred jobs that are rough and humble
and I would have liked a trade where you get really thick-skinned hands
with lots of calluses, I'd have been proud to have hands like that.' His
art has no pretensions to being beautiful or valuable—it is one of supreme
indigence. Chaissac works with the most commonplace materials, assembling
his objects from old pots and pans, sieves, brooms, discarded shoes, leather
scraps, bottles, trowels and spades, bits of fencing, roots, bricks, stones.
His preference seems to be for things that have already *done service* and
thus have a mysterious negative value. When he paints, he very rarely
uses canvas, but applies his colours to blotting paper, corrugated cardboard, wallpaper—where the traditionally 'best' surface is not available,
he turns to the next best, which means any surface within reach. His colours
are anything but recherché—he likes silver and garish reds; he makes use
of charcoal and chalk, and smothers his objects with scraps of coloured
paper. His unproblematical attitude towards technique makes Benjamin
Péret call him a 'popular dandy'—at the opposite pole from urban aestheticism, Chaissac's rural dandysm means attachment to the primitive roughness
of things, and an ironical coolness on the topic of financial success. 'I once
thought of setting up a shop to sell bath-tubs in a region where people
never took a bath, since at all events I'm in favour of failing in all enter-
prises.' A serene complicity with failure is perhaps the secret of Chaissac's
art, which, totally indifferent to academic standards, lacks the 'finished'
look of art-without-wrinkles. Chaissac once explained: 'As I could never
sketch things except in a gaunt and scraggy way, I stressed my clumsiness
whenever I could, having noticed that the more my drawing was botched,
the less it had that rigid art-student look.' Happily botched, Chaissac's
creations are the product of a spontaneity that is, as Jakovsky points out,
a far cry from the testy methodicality of the naïve painter. His festive masks
and tragi-comic totems transmit a pulse that is far from regular. Devoid of
all cultural trimmings and artifice, Chaissac's art is, in Dubuffet's dry
words, 'not much of a meal for the art critics of the Ecole de Paris'.

Gaston Chaissac *Totem* 1961
Collection Rossi, courtesy Iris Clert

N° 247   10-8-1944   Crépin Fr JB

Joseph Crépin Painting no. 247, 1944
Galerie les Deux Iles, Paris

Clarence Schmidt House

Bogosav Zivković *Head of a liar* detail
from a column
Reproduced from *Bogosav Živković* by
O. Bihalji-Merin, by kind permission of
Jugoslavija Editions

Bogosav Živković Small column with
human figure riding a pig
Reproduced from *Bogosav Živković* by
O. Bihalji-Merin, by kind permission of
Jugoslavija Editions

Opposite
Laure Pigeon Drawing dated
11 June 1954
Collection de l'Art Brut, Paris,
courtesy Jean Dubuffet

Laure Pigeon Drawing dated
15 December 1961
Collection de l'Art Brut, Paris,
courtesy Jean Dubuffet

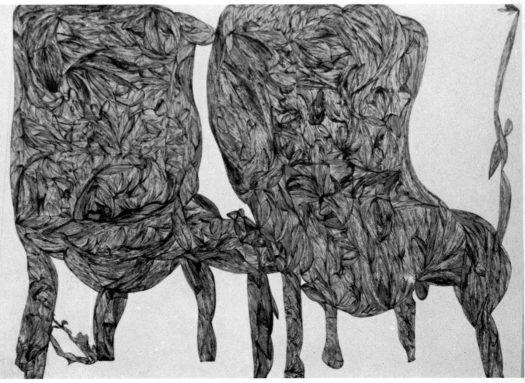

Johann Knüpfer *Glory of my Saviour*
Prinzhorn collection, Heidelberg

Aloïse *Waterloo/Marie Stuart/Werder/Tosca* 1942
Reproduced from *Though this be madness (Insania pingens)* by A. Bader, H.
Steck, G. Schmidt, J. Cocteau (Thames and Hudson, London 1961), by
kind permission of Dr Alfred Bader

Ferdinand Cheval
Bizarre stone
on the terrace
of the Palais idéal

Ferdinand Cheval Tomb

Madge Gill 1884–1961

In an article in the magazine *Prediction* (1937), the mediumistic artist Madge Gill is quoted as follows:

> It was in 1919 when I first started my work. I then had an inspiration to take up my pen and do all kinds of work of an artistic type. I felt that I had an artistic faculty seeking expression. It took various forms. First of all, knitting—even doing pieces of knitting on one knitting needle without any pattern. Then came a flow of all kinds of inspirational writing, mostly Biblical.
>
> Then I felt impelled to execute drawings on a large scale on calico. I simply couldn't leave it and I did on average 20 pictures a week, all in colour. All the time I was in quite a normal state of mind and there was no suggestion of a 'spirit' standing beside me. I simply felt inspired. Sometimes I would be dissatisfied with the work and tear it up or burn it. But I felt I was definitely guided by an unseen force, though I could not say what its actual nature was.

Maude Ethel Eades was born in the Great Portland Street area in London in 1884. Her early life remains obscure: she was illegitimate (her father may have been a portrait painter called Sargent, living in Blackheath), and was looked after by her mother and her aunt Carrie for a while until she could be placed in a children's home. Eventually she was sent to Canada, and did not return until the age of nineteen, when she took a job as a nurse in Whipps Cross Hospital, London. She lived at this time in Ilford in the house of her aunt Kate, who, as a 'great believer' in spiritualism, introduced her to séances and fortune telling. Here she met her cousin Thomas Gill, a stockbroker's clerk, who felt sorry for the way life had treated her. The two were married in 1907, and lived in a succession of homes in the East End of London. Three sons were born, of whom the second, Reggie, was to die at the age of eight in the 1918 influenza epidemic. This tragedy was soon followed by another when Mrs Gill, whose mind had been set on having a daughter, gave birth to a stillborn girl. She herself almost died, and remained ill for several months, finally losing the sight of her left eye, which had to be replaced with a glass one. It was now that she took up drawing and painting, often working at night in bed by the light of an oil lamp, and perhaps even in total darkness. She had become, according to her son Laurie, a true medium in contact with a spirit guide:

> It was on March 3rd. 1920 when the now medium was taken in a trance and controlled by a very progressed Spirit, whom we now know as MYRNINEREST her Guide. All that day the medium was in a trance

Madge Gill Figure in geometrical setting 1954
Newham (London) collection, courtesy James Green

and as no one in the domestic circle knew what Spiritualism meant, it caused great awe at the time. However from that day until the present time the Inspiration has been one true reality, in every stage of it. . . . Spiritual or Inspirational Drawings, Writings, Speaking, Singing, Inspired Piano Playing, making knitted woollen clothes and weaving silk Mats in beautifully blended colours.

Laurie's broadsheet *MYRNINEREST The Spheres*, issued in 1926, gives a more spectacular version of things than did Mrs Gill in 1937. He may have the date wrong (he was only in his early teens in 1920), and it may be that the idea of the spirit guide was concocted by his mother for home consumption, since in public she stresses the lack of such a spirit. Yet the fact of a sudden prolific upsurge of creativity is clear, and there are impressive examples of Mrs Gill's embroidery and knitting still extant apart from her drawings and writings. (It was Laurie who excelled at piano improvisations.)

Circumstances did indeed encourage Madge Gill's preoccupation with her imaginative work. She got on badly with her husband, who spent a lot of time with other women; when her son Bob was injured in a motorbike accident, and was bedridden for two years, she frequently sat up nights at his side, working at her drawings. After Thomas Gill died of cancer in 1933, she continued to keep house for her two sons of whom she was very fond; for the few years till his death, her brother-in-law Bert also lived with them. He it was who communicated an interest in astrology to Bob and thence to the rest of the family. By the mid-thirties, Madge Gill had extended the scope of her spiritualist activities, holding weekly séances in her house which involved table-turnings and the ouija-board. She is known to have cast horoscopes for friends, drawing up elaborate astrological charts in red and black inks.

In the thirties, Mrs Gill attracted attention in the press when she exhibited some of her larger works at the East End Academy. But rarely did she part with any pieces, and she always refused to sell. A large fabric shown at a wartime show in 1942 was marked £1000, no doubt an intentionally unrealistic price. In 1947, after exhibiting again at the East End Academy, she is reported as having turned down the offer of a West End show. In general she shunned publicity, and explained her unwillingness to sell by saying that the pictures were not hers, but the property of her spirit guide.

The name MYRNINEREST appears on a high percentage of her drawings, usually accompanied by a cross. Probably Mrs Gill relied on this signature from another realm as a means of justifying the intensity of an activity which kept her from sleeping, and which was not always pleasurable. Often she would work through the night at feverish speed, standing up in front of one of the large rolls of calico which Laurie fitted up for her in a special frame so that it could be unwound and worked bit by bit. The compulsion to create was at times worrying to her sons, who feared for her health. The spirit guide, one imagines, was a dramatic way of referring to the unseen force which she experienced to some extent as a burden. In a note apparently addressed to a woman friend in 1952, is this confession: 'Man directs his efforts in the trend of thoughts which scoop through the brain. The crust of the earth, beneath lies untold wealth, so it is with the mastermind true genius will out. Dear Louise, I wish I could be normal.' Mrs Gill was probably half-aware of the source of this outburst of genius, and one might surmise that the word 'Myrninerest' means 'mine innerest self'.

In later life, Madge Gill took to drinking heavily and had a certain reputation in her neighbourhood as a nice old lady when sober, but a terrible woman when drunk. Many considered her a crank, and she no doubt encouraged this with odd mannerisms such as suddenly looking people straight in the eye and rattling off a spontaneous prediction, that in some cases would come true. She went on drawing until 1958, by which time she had outlived her son Bob, and was living alone with Laurie in a large and gloomy house in Plashet Grove, East Ham. Both were ill. When she died in 1961 at the age of seventy-seven, she left hundreds of drawings in the house, piled in wardrobes or under beds, many torn or damaged by damp.

The largest of Madge Gill's works are done on rolls of calico bought at the local draper's at 2¾d a yard. The large fabric entitled *The Crucifixion of the Soul* measures about five by thirty-five feet. These 'tapestry' pictures are scarcely less intricate in detail than her smallest pieces, and her clarity of touch is remarkable. What is most astonishing is the overall sense of harmony, given that she never saw the complete fabric while working on it. Many are in black indian ink, which is rarely smudged. Others are in coloured inks: blue, green and yellow, with colours such as mauve and orange presumably obtained by mixing. A considerable part of her output consists of pictures done on cardboard, again in coloured inks; on many of these she carefully noted the date of commencement and completion.

Madge Gill Composition 1951 on reverse 'Reggie passed away 1918 October 27 Born 27 April 1910'
Collection de l'Art Brut, Paris, courtesy Jean Dubuffet

Madge Gill Veiled face
Newham (London) collection, courtesy James Green

From this it is clear that she usually had several pictures on hand at any one time. There are extremely few pictures which are not fully completed; one exceptional piece on a very long roll of paper peters out after a while, and reveals that her practice, at least here, was to sketch out a basic design in very free arabesques, thereafter to decorate the areas thus outlined with concentrated care. Nearly all her drawings are in ink, though there are a few experiments in crayons and oils. There also exist hundreds of postcards, many dated and signed 'Myrninerest', sometimes produced at the rate of a dozen in an evening. Many of these have writing on the back—notes of public events or private thoughts ('Armistice Day', 'Vesuvius in eruption', 'The harbour lights ahead Break waters', 'Wallace Collection of Beautiful Portrait Paintings', 'Cancer Cure'), and fragmentary ideas drawn from her spiritualist and astrological reading (references to Christ's divine mission;

Madge Gill *Mars*
Newham (London) collection, courtesy James Green

to the inhabitants of Mars; to Adepts and the migration of Souls, zodiac stones, etc.). There are also messages from her spirit guide in the form of exhortations to sustain her perseverance and courage. From time to time these inscriptions contain smatterings of imperfect French, and even merge into sequences of apparent nonsense, in which the artist undoubtedly took delight. One of her least characteristic colour drawings consists of a criss-cross pattern with little squares that looks like a board for some abstruse game, and may be some form of astrological chart. In the squares are set the following verbal elements, in which proper names and bits of French are mixed with pure neologisms:

> Myrninerest Mars/Mars canals/Vedi/dai/My all/ Jupiter luminary
> planet/through wireless Master mind/Saturn Vercois lenario supio/
> Dante's Ergo line 8 Communication Valloisère French Ambassador/
> Lesto du maoi lexiem stellation/Welingoi/Dante/Mascoise/Leoix
> Weil/Vellos maileo plane/pleot du/Mend thy ways/Plane vex/lallex all
> Noel/Du sangeo/Masteo Valloice/un Jour faith to the Cross.*

As well as linguistic play, there are doodles which look like an experimental shorthand or a 'Martian' calligraphy like that developed by the medium Helen Smith. But if these pseudo-signs lack semantic meaning, they still have pictographic significance: the squiggles, crosses and zigzags that fill the spaces in her drawings are not a meaningless scribbling but a coherent artistic handwriting of considerable emotional force.

Apart from notes added to her drawings, there exist a few literary sketches, mainly 'inspirational writings' couched in a style which, for all its neglect of spelling and punctuation and futile repetitiveness, has its very expressive moments. In one text she refers to Dante, and speaks of the grotesque shapes of trees that can produce fear in an imaginative mind—apparently an allusion to the opening of the *Inferno*. Another sketch evidently constituted part of a story in the form of a dramatic monologue that focuses on a scene in a crowded courtroom in which a divorce suit is being heard. The woman whose thoughts are recorded recoils from the venomous tongues around her, and bemoans the mental cruelty inflicted by her husband, who had rejected the girl-child she bore him as being an insult to his family lineage. This piece bears the usual signature of Myrninerest. Her other prose includes a Biblical text in florid handwriting entitled 'Second Coming of Jesus Christ' and a confused essay on high finance

* This transcription from the picture in the Newham Collection is subject to omissions and mis-transcriptions, owing to the difficulty of deciphering Madge Gill's handwriting.

Madge Gill Three draped figures in chequered setting ('The three sisters')
dated 8 October 1952
Newham (London) collection, courtesy James Green

signed Lord Rothschild. . . .

Madge Gill's main achievement clearly lies in her pictorial work. Typical of her imagery is the repeated feminine figure with its stereotyped nose and mouth in an oval face, and large eyes, often shaded by a hat or masked from direct view by cross-hatching. These faces proliferate, especially in the large fabrics: I have counted over a hundred in the large one in the art brut collection. One recognizes a timid girl with a tight hat in the twenties manner; at times this hat is larger, and is adorned with graceful feathers. Can this creature be Madge Gill as a young woman? Could it be an image of her lost mother? Or of the daughter that was unable to grow up? Sentimental speculations of this kind may point vaguely at a complex psychic truth; certainly one can find no male figures around.

Though hands and arms are occasionally seen, the tendency is for the feminine figure to be robed in flowing garments that merge into the surrounding design, in a way that denies any clear contour to the body. Indeed, the figure often appears to be perfectly suspended between being a shape in its own right and a form utterly absorbed in the ambient pattern. The background tends to impose itself as the sphere of major attention. It usually consists of a labyrinth of chequered areas of varying shape, filled in with a great variety of devices—spirals, wavy lines, cobwebs, crosses, dots, zigzags, circles, etc. These areas are set in conflict by a deliberate avoidance of strict 'perspective' or other form of balance. Where the eye seeks some measure of architectural stability—for one feels led to 'read' the designs as architecture, the chequered patterns as tiled floors, the vertical strokes as pillars, the curved arcs as the archways of some fantastic palace—it is constantly thwarted by being diverted into new directions. The effect is one of such insistent reorientation that the conscious viewer who seeks to recognize structures congruent with established notions of artistic design—harmony, symmetry, conventional Gestalt—will feel highly frustrated. Whereas, to a less intellectually attentive gaze, the oscillation between abstraction and representation, and the vibration of the patterns, create a tension that is highly stimulating. The space projected in these drawings is mimetic of the mental trajectory that the artist followed: no longer more than a perfunctory acknowledgment of external space, it may be considered in quite literal terms as the delineation of a private world, a realm of subjective fantasy rendered concrete in the act of figuration. In a strange literary sketch that reads like an artistic confession, Mrs Gill writes:

Deep down in the heart of every human being there lies the soul with its longing yearning after the attainable, but at what a cost to the unrecognized individual who strikes out after originality.

Imperfect speech impartial knowledge unsophisticated uneducated yet to a degree of insufferable uncongeniality if desires are studied first, one must always remain the third person if feelings are to be exonerated.

The passage indicates her awareness of her artistic gifts, and her conviction of the originality of her vision. Though she remained hesitant in her prose, being embarrassed by her inadequate control over the usual medium of sophisticated exchange, she was able in her 'inspired' drawings to create a highly articulate style of her own. Madge Gill did indeed manage to 'exonerate her feelings' by remaining the discreet 'third person'—placing her emotions in the objective space of the picture, where her desires might no longer be subject to the uncertainties and tragedies of the drab existence in which she found herself.

See also illustration page 41.

Ferdinand Cheval 1836–1924

The Palais idéal built by the postman Ferdinand Cheval is hidden away off the main street of the French village of Hauterives, about halfway between Lyon and Romans. It is an eccentric structure that can vie with any of the follies produced in England in the eighteenth century or with the ornate art nouveau buildings of Gaudi in Barcelona. So wide a range of apparent influences and original departures does it embody that it offers something for everyone, and usually dictates a lyrical and delirious style to anyone that writes about it. In their book *Fantastic architecture*, Ulrich Conrad and Hans Sperlich write: 'Half pagoda, half robber-baron's castle, half nymphaeum, half tomb; not Baroque, not Hellenistic, not Buddhist, not Indian, and yet all of them at once. In a breath-taking way and with the tenacity of movement and the seemingly shackled logic of the dream, differences in time and space are bridged.' While it is hard to resist the contagion of this sort of enthusiasm, it might be well to begin more soberly, more flatly, taking Cheval's own prose style as a cue for some plain facts.

Cheval, the self-styled 'obscure hero', was born at Charmes, near Romans, in 1836, and received a very sparse education. After his marriage, he worked for a while as a baker. It was in about 1864, one gathers, that he had the dream that was to affect his whole life. In this dream, he saw himself constructing a palace, or a castle, or grottoes—he was unable to express the picturesque details of the vision, though it remained imprinted on his memory as something wonderful. For the time being he did nothing about it. It was at about this time that Cheval went for a short while to Algeria, probably on military service, an exceptional experience for someone who otherwise scarcely left his native region. It would indeed be interesting to know whether he had his dream before or after this journey, so as to assess whether the exoticism of Northern Africa affected the shaping of the original 'ideal palace'. Shortly after he returned from abroad, Cheval's wife died. He re-married, and became a postman, firstly part-time, then full-time, covering thirty-two kilometres a day on his cross-country round between the villages of the Drôme. His job gave him plenty of time to day-dream, and he probably elaborated his fantasy palace as he trudged along. He tells us that he had gradually given up this reverie, though, when one day in 1879 he tripped on a stone and bent down to pick it up. The stone had been weathered through the ages to form a kind of natural sculpture, and was of such a bizarre and suggestive shape that he put it in his pocket so as to admire it at leisure that evening. Next day Cheval returned to the same place and found yet finer specimens, which he piled up for gradual transportation to his home. 'Since Nature wants to be the sculptor', he thought, 'I shall be the mason and the architect'. His life's work began on this impulse, and he started to bring in stones from dry riverbeds or the roadside every day, piling them up in his garden in preparation for his work. It was in the previous year that Cheval's only daughter Alice had been born, and Anatole Jakovsky suggests that the joy he felt at having this late-born child may have something to do with this sudden decision to erect some kind of lasting monument, perhaps in her honour. Alternatively one may prefer to think that his sudden inspiration was a force that had lain potential for a long period, being simply released by the accidental encounter with the stone.

'From dreams to reality is a long way', reflected Cheval, who had never touched a trowel in his life, and had not the slightest notion of the principles of architecture. Yet the working methods he developed over the years were equal to the colossal task of transforming a vision into a mass of stone and cement weighing many tons. Cheval's materials were drawn from the region around Hauterives, which, being once an ocean bed, is rich in calcareous tufa, a spongy limestone which takes on all kinds of shapes, as well as actual fossils. Cheval brought these home in his pockets, until his wife complained of the tears, after which he used baskets; later he made excursions with a wheelbarrow in the evening after work, going round to pick up the piles he had left in various places, and often covering colossal distances. His affection for his tools, and for the wheelbarrow in particular is evinced in a crude poem in honour of his 'faithful companion'. To supplement the found materials, Cheval had to buy cement and lime and metal wire, and invented a kind of reinforced concrete, modelling the wet mix over a metal skeleton with considerable skill. Into this he would press small pebbles, fossils or shells, or else apply tree-bark to impart a texture. 'Gossip then began in the district,' writes Cheval in one of his notebooks, 'and it was not long before the opinion of the locality was established: "There's a poor mad fool filling up his garden with stones." Indeed, people were quite prepared to believe it was a case of sick imagination. People laughed, disapproved, and criticized me, but as this sort of alienation was neither contagious nor dangerous, they didn't see much point in fetching the doctor, and I was thus able to give myself up to my passion in perfect liberty in spite of it all.' The postman was upheld by a peasant stubbornness and pride, and by immense powers of endurance; he would frequently work at night with a candle on his hat, and never failed to complete his delivery-round by day. For thirty-three years he toiled on, getting through four thousand sacks of lime and cement and tons of stones, intent only that something lasting should be the result. Again and again he stresses his conviction that all this work cannot fail to assure him a lasting place in people's memories. The Palais idéal has lasted, and is indeed, in terms of sheer size and effort, an unrivalled achievement. It covers a total area of

Ferdinand Cheval Palais idéal—the Three Giants and the Tower of Barbary

about twenty-six by fourteen metres, and varies between eight and ten metres in height; the details are meticulously recorded in Cheval's accounts of his work.

At an early stage in the building, Cheval dug out a vault three metres deep, in which he hoped to be buried some day 'in the manner of the Pharaohs'. Down below are two stone coffins, and above a heavily ornamented temple. Alain Borne concludes that it was his literal intention to be buried here, so that his body should accompany his fame into the future. He deduces that the authorities must have refused Cheval permission to carry out this plan.

On the other side of this east façade, is a crypt containing Cheval's trusty tools: the wheelbarrow, the mixing-bucket, the trowel. Nearby rise up the Three Giants, Vercingetorix, Archimedes and Caesar, the guardians

Ferdinand Cheval Detail of north façade of the Palais idéal

of the Palace. They are tall figures of lime and sand encrusted with red
and blue-grey flints, and are considered by Cheval to be 'somewhat in
the Egyptian manner'. Between these stand two smaller female figures,
the Druidesses Veleda and Iniza. The north façade, though smaller, is
no less interesting, and is perhaps the most fascinating part of the Palace
from the sculptural point of view. It consists of a number of little grottoes
over which hang layers of little animals assembled from tufa and stones
found in the river: pelicans, ducks, deer, rams, piglets, crocodiles, and
extending upwards to form a bristling silhouette.

Cheval spent twenty years or so on these first two façades, which are his
finest work. The other two took him only about twelve years. The south
façade is comparatively insipid, and the west façade is spoiled by a number
of inept attempts to pay homage to architectural styles that Cheval had

learnt about from popular magazines. The Hindu temple, the Swiss chalet, the White House, the Algerian House, the Medieval Castle, these are painstaking set-pieces of a vulgarity that is in sad contrast to the originality and verve of the earlier façades. One is tempted to say that Cheval was filling-in for the sake of it, though he genuinely felt he was perfecting his masterpiece, and apparently remained oblivious of the let-down one feels when one walks from the front to the back of the Palace.

'Entrée d'un palais imaginaire'—the inscription on the 'mosque' to the right of the west façade invites the visitor to explore the inner chambers of the Palace, which Cheval called the 'hetacombs'. As in some underground passage only dimly lit from outside, one walks past walls covered with vaguely mythological scenes in semi-relief, with flying birds, bears, elephants, shepherds and other figures, described by Cheval as 'so bizarre that one might think one were in a dream'. At either end of the central passage are vaulted ceilings bearing chandeliers of stone, ringed with dozens of shells and fossil snails. On the terrace above, reached by staircases at three corners of the Palace, one can view the total edifice, and even climb higher, up the Tower of Barbary with its 'oasis' of palm trees and cacti in cement.

The complexity of the building is augmented by the large number of inscriptions in the form of mottoes or poems. Some proudly acclaim the energy of the creator: 'In the minutes of leisure/allowed by my employment/I built this Palace/of a Thousand and One Nights/wherein I have engraved my memory.' The task was assuredly daunting, yet 'Nothing is impossible/To the valiant heart', and Cheval does not hesitate to extol his achievement: 'This marvel, whose author may be proud,/Shall be unique in the universe.' Some inscriptions are in a sombre metaphysical vein: 'On this earth/Like shadows we pass./Coming from dust,/To dust we shall return.' Or again: 'Life is an ocean full of storms/Between the child just born/And the old man soon to vanish.' While Cheval constantly harps on his humble background: 'All that you see, passer-by,/Is the work of a peasant', he sees his work as a transcendence of these origins: 'From the sources of life/I have drawn my genius.' Some of the inscriptions attain an authentic poetry, as in the phrase 'Where dream becomes reality', and the enigmatic 'From a dream I have brought forth/The queen of the world'—a hint at a 'feminine' element in the inspiration which may be associated with either Madame Cheval or his daughter.

A plain explanation of the creative process operating in the Palais idéal is difficult, for Cheval's own explanations, recorded in a few notebooks, are, despite the facts he gives, generally evasive when it comes to saying *why* he felt so urgent a duty to create. The story of the dream may not satisfy everyone. In her book *Opium and the Romantic Imagination*, Alethea Hayter refers to the Palais idéal as a splendid instance of the creative impulse being sparked off by a dream, in the manner of Coleridge's poem *Kubla Khan*, with its evocation of the pleasure-dome at Xanadu. 'It was his paradise, the world in which he wished to live, to sleep', she lyricizes. Certainly Cheval's work has the dual function, serving as absorbing extension of the man while he was alive, and as a monument to his memory after death. But why was the dream so compelling as to keep Cheval at work for so long?

There exists, according to Jakovsky, a drawing made by a known medium and neighbour of Cheval's, Cadier, which depicts the Palais idéal. Certain discrepancies between the drawing and the building may indicate the former was in fact the point of departure from which Cheval diverged as his work progressed. Unproven though this theory is, it gives some credence to André Breton's assertion that 'the postman Cheval remains the undisputed master of mediumistic sculpture and architecture'. Whether or not Cheval had revelations of a mediumistic kind himself—and in Breton's terms these would be perfectly equated with the notion of automatism, or inspiration projected from the unconscious—there is a note of authenticity in Breton's suggestion that Cheval must have been 'haunted' by the stalactite formations in the grottoes of the Drôme region.

It is perfectly clear that Cheval derived a good many ideas from other sources than his individual imagination. In his mature years he certainly tried to make up for his lack of education by reading odd books and illustrated magazines like *Le Magasin pittoresque*. The west façade is a rather self-conscious publicization of the knowledge he gained about foreign parts, though the inaccuracies in his version of exotic architectural styles are flagrant; the Algiers house, for example, being more like a wedding-cake than anything else. Evidently Cheval grew attracted to the idea of methodical setting-out of recognizable items, and his disposition of geological specimens and rows of sculptures are reminiscent of a museum. As such, the Palace covers geology, botany, and zoology, and constitutes a kind of naïve summary of the wonders of the world. In this respect Cheval's work might seem to veer towards becoming a perfectly *cultural* work (a tendency encouraged by its present administration by the Musée des Beaux-Arts and the swarms of tourists). But what there is in it of naïve and therefore harmless exoticism (what Borne calls its Jules Verne side), is compensated by a 'raw' strangeness, that remains, on the whole, the stronger impression. If the Palace is a parade of half-digested bits of information about the world beyond Hauterives, it remains interesting precisely because they *are* only half-digested. If this is so, the work becomes not a universal museum of checked facts, but an imaginary reconstruction of the world. Thanks to isolation and ignorance, perhaps also to a solid crust of peasant obstinacy, little real culture got through to Cheval, so that his creation may finally be valid as, to quote Jacques Brunius, 'a monstrous system of imagined memories', rather than actual ones.

As a total design, the Palace is grotesque and ill-balanced. The test of 'organic unity' would demonstrate almost complete recalcitrance to aesthetic standards. The Palace is *not* a thing of beauty, nor a harmonious whole. Where one can see signs of an attempt to make something beautiful, these have resulted in mere naïve Prettiness. As a block of discrepant parts, the Palace is splendidly anarchic and refuses symmetry to an extent quite exceptional in a work of architecture. All the same there *is* something coherent about it, and one might grope towards defining this as the overall 'feel' of the place, corresponding to the creator's personality, perhaps. In certain lights, the deadness of the stone can be forgotten as the sculpted animals and plants assert their own life. The proliferation of sprouting forms produces a dynamism that Borne attributes to the preponderance of sexual symbols—vaginal grottoes and niches, rows of breasts, phallic stalagmites, branches and minarets. In this light, the Palace becomes a monstrous symbol of orgiastic copulation, the artistic sublimation of a frustrated male desire. But this is to press too heavily on the Freudian pedal. The remedy is to extend the insight through wider associations, and, remembering Cheval's own idea that Nature was his collaborator, to envisage the work as a kind of hymn to the boundless fecundity of natural functions—and therefore, in the last analysis, as a celebration of something non-civilised, regressive, primeval. Brunius' delirious development of the theme is hard to resist:

> In detail his labours consisted in recreating in his medium of cement, the forms of nature of all kinds. Men, animals or plants spring up as though transfixed in life, out of a setting or background which one can also recognize itself to be composed of innumerable organic forms, mineral, vegetable, animal, comestible: boiling pools of lava, boulders, concretions of chalky grottoes, meteorites, pebbles, oyster shells, shellfish themselves, agglomerations of giant animalculae, enormous worms—a whole morphology of marine existence, polypods and sponges, then clusters of intestines, fossilized logs, petrified fountains, leaves of acanthus, sea-weed, caviar, vermicelli, puddings, and all kinds of excrement—and so on in infinite variety of reminiscence.

Is this the net result of Cheval's monument—to summon us to an intuition of life as natural growth, to respond to the pulse of an extra-human vitality, in which is transcended our civilized fear of stepping into life and stepping into death?

Cheval completed his Palais idéal in 1912, and spent a couple of years pottering around, clearing up the site, planting a garden and proudly showing visitors around. But all was not yet accomplished: he had yet to construct a resting-place where he would be allowed to lie. Somehow Cheval was allowed a more or less free hand to erect a fantastic tomb in a corner right by the entrance to the village cemetery (see page 131). Work began in 1914, and took eight years. One might have expected something conventional of a man in his eighties, and parts of the Palais idéal would not be too conspicuous in the average French cemetery. But Cheval felt no compulsion to conform to the context. Now master of his medium, he contorts his wire-and-cement shapes into a mass of interwoven lianas that tumble and thrust in ungainly yet muscular rhythms. Borne calls the work a final explosion of sexuality, the apotheosis of a delirium of compensation. But the tomb has a ghastly lugubriousness, partly caused by its 'tasteless' coat of red paint; and one recoils from it as from an inhuman celebration of death—it is a *Totentanz* of macabre power, scarcely contained within the four sides of the plot of ground allocated to Cheval.

When he died in 1924, at the age of eighty-eight, Cheval was buried beneath this writhing mass, which he had called 'the tomb of silence and endless rest'. Apparently without completely realizing it, he had managed to create two highly moving works that owe their greatest effect to their creator's not having had the education that he consciously regretted having missed. These masterpieces establish themselves outside of any rigid classification. Is the Palais idéal architecture or sculpture, mausoleum or museum? It invites us to say that it is all these and more, and, if a label is needed, it merits nothing less than the one given by Brunius: 'a monument to the imagination'.

See also illustrations page 134.

Friedrich Schröder-Sonnenstern
1892–

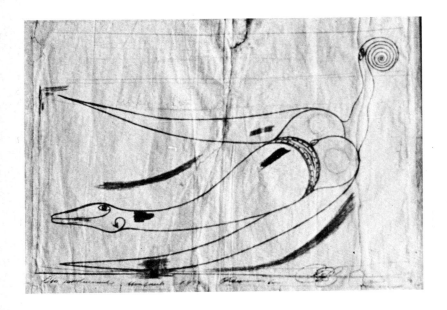

Friedrich Schröder-Sonnenstern Drawing
Galerie Hilt, Basle

The life of Friedrich Schröder-Sonnenstern exemplifies the refusal to conform. The son of a Lithuanian coachman, he grew up as an obstinate outsider amongst thirteen children, sharpening his sense of individuality by ferocious pranks directed at his companions. After attending a reform school at the age of fourteen, he had a succession of menial country jobs. On one occasion he was falsely accused of stealing and resisted police arrest with a knife, which behaviour earned him five months' internment in a lunatic asylum. When called up to fight in the war, he put on such a display of idiocy that the authorities confirmed his mental deficiency and declared him unfit for service. Towards the end of the war he was interned as a dangerous lunatic, and subjected to very harsh treatment. During the inter-war years, Schröder-Sonnenstern dabbled in mysticism and astrology, spent some time in prison, and ended up in the ruins of postwar Berlin living in the cellar of a bombed house. In 1949, at the age of fifty-seven, he began to produce drawings in coloured pencils, and eventually became established as an artist.

Schröder-Sonnenstern's art is one of scandal and derisive caricature that assaults the social prejudices and sexual taboos that are the props of civilized man. The directness of his attack has something flamboyant about it; yet it cannot be maintained that his association with commercial galleries is proof of mental dependence or a thirst for publicity at any cost. Some may discern signs of a certain complacency in his symmetrical neatness, a fey charm in his humorous grotesqueries. But whilst he is not as free of influences as some of the other artists in this book, Schröder-Sonnenstern's lucid alienation expresses itself without appreciable cultural compromise, conveying a sufficiently intense disgust for 'the gangrene of civilization' to silence charges of latent aestheticism. His declaration of independence is quite admirable: 'You have smashed my hopes, gagged my spirit, tortured my soul, and now, stinking brood, you want me to vote for you—I vote for *myself.*'

Raymond Isidore 1900–64

Raymond Isidore was born in the cathedral city of Chartres in 1900. He had little education, and certainly no artistic training. His job was that of sweeper in the cemetery; his spare time was spent building a house on a plot he had bought in the rue du Repos, in a humble quarter near the cemetery. In 1928 he married, and within a few years had begun to decorate his house and garden. The idea of doing so had come to him, he says, when he had picked up some bright bits of broken porcelain and glass while going for a walk in the fields. Isidore collected such fragments—shattered plates, medicine bottles, mirrors, plaster roses off old graves—and set to work to encrust his habitation in an all-pervading mosaic. He was acting, he thought, under the influence of some sort of higher power, and would dream each night of the work to be done next day—sometimes getting so excited that he got up to work in the dark. As the years went by, the whole property was gradually covered over: the house, the outhouses, the yard, the paths, the high walls that enclose the private space of the garden. There are two large thrones, a tomb and a shrine, a decorated tree and a number of standing sculptures made in cement. About the house and garden are distributed over a hundred large flowerpots inlaid with mosaic. Inside the house, the compulsion to decorate has overtaken each last surface—the cupboards, the tables, even the sewing-machine. The kitchen chairs are almost too heavy to use. After some thirty-three years' work, Isidore relaxed and enjoyed the satisfaction of a completed task, before he died in 1964. 'I have arrived at my destination', he declared in 1962, 'a place that suits my taste, my beliefs, a place where I can feel at liberty, even if it doesn't appeal to everybody, just so long as it pleases me and my wife.' With his Maison Picassiette, he had achieved an environment precisely adequate to his emotional needs.

Isidore's method was to prepare a portion of his surface with wet cement and then rapidly insert the fragments of material before it dried. One might imagine that the need to make haste and the lack of any preliminary diagram would have resulted in a certain improvised haphazardness. In fact the ornamental designs consistently repeat the same rigid patterns: the rose-window shape, the five-petalled flower, the eight-pointed star. The scenes represented are not original: the influence of picture postcards and of the stained glass windows of Chartres cathedral is obvious. Isidore's flowers, dogs, butterflies, horses and stiff human figures are the work of a naïf—the fresco paintings on the garden wall are particularly weak, the 'copy' of the Mona Lisa pathetic. Isidore's religious or folklore images may be grandiose in intention, but their effect is simply banal. Thus it is that one may feel the temptation to ignore the actual contours of the cathedrals and the people, slackening one's focus till the 'figure' is overcome, as it

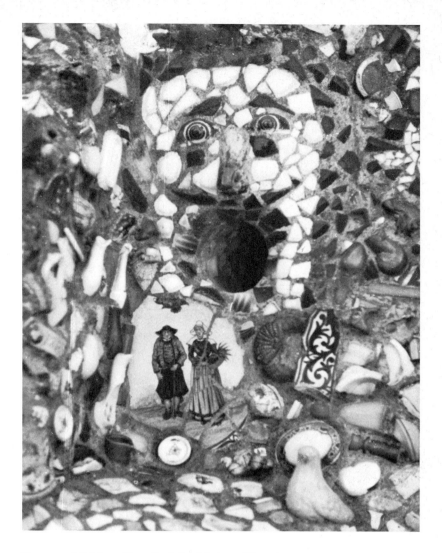

Raymond Isidore Detail of the Maison Picassiette

easily is, by the 'ground' of the fragmented surface of the mosaic. Then the effect of dancing shards of interacting colour particles can prompt a kaleido-scopic impression that is euphoric and dynamic, something that is not available at the static level of Gestalt-recognition. Or again one can, in some corners of the garden, peer closely and discover the original designs and even words on the broken crockery, enjoying their unintended juxta-positions. Brought close to the appeal of the *material* in all its splendid poverty and dissonance, one can sense the original thrill of a primary creativity that was—so one realizes on stepping back again—spoiled by the over-geometrical attentions of the secondary, reflective process. Seen in this light, Isidore's work illustrates the imposition of a disappointingly re-strictive harmonic principle upon potentially fertile raw material.

Karl Brendel 1871–?

Born into a large Thuringian family in 1871, Karl Brendel was an intelligent and equable child who did well at school. He became a mason, and may later have done stucco work, travelling about the country. In 1895 he married a widow who had three children, and the marriage produced two more. But in 1902 his wife obtained a divorce, apparently as the outcome of a number of prison sentences that Brendel had incurred on charges including offensive behaviour, committing bodily harm and wilful destruction of property. Having badly injured his left leg in 1900, Brendel later had to undergo a series of operations that finally led to its amputation. He launched a querulous campaign against the authorities to obtain full compensation for this. In 1906 manifest symptoms of a chronic hallucinatory psychosis led to his commission to a mental hospital. He had auditory hallucinations, imagining that a ventriloquist was conversing with him, and delusions of reference whereby he attributed aggressive intentions to anything moving near his person. He claimed that he was pursued by a mermaid who followed him about in the garden, that people tried to poison him, that electrical shocks were passing through his body. To him, all these phenomena seemed quite real. In conversation he would range far and wide over all sorts of topics, in a mannered but forceful style of speech which, though incoherent, had its moments of true wit. He was an unreliable patient and during his agitated spells had to be kept in isolation (he once hit a visiting clergyman). Prinzhorn records his impression of a big strong fellow who hopped around on one leg with great agility, and supplemented his talk with vigorous movements of his body, suggestive of deep sexual drives. He was, says Prinzhorn, a man who expressed himself forcibly, and one could appreciate that five wardens were needed to tackle him when he was in a rage. This expressive force comes across in Brendel's art, that of a man who likes to exert his strength upon physical objects.

Brendel's writings are a parade of long and involved explanations concerning the loss of his leg, his struggle to get compensation, his bitterness towards the clergy (who apparently failed to help him when he was in hospital), his admiration for the surgeon who had treated him, and allusions to his marriage. The texts are difficult to understand, because of Brendel's atrophied grammar, which suppresses all linking words and runs ideas together according to the haphazard dictates of association. Apart from some drawings, Brendel's main achievements are his carvings, usually carried out on large blocks of hard and heavy wood which one imagines was very difficult to work. Many pieces are painted or varnished, and show considerable technical confidence, despite Brendel's lack of artistic tuition (previous to his internment, he had carved toys for his children, and made a few picture-frames). Inspiration came spontaneously: no external model was used, and indeed the stylized animals and caricatural figures are evidence of a deliberate will to shape non-realistic forms, to project objects of the imagination. Brendel's own explanation of his urge to create stresses the affective factor: 'When I have a block of wood in front of me, then there's a hypnosis in it—if I give in, something comes of it—otherwise there's a conflict.'

One of Brendel's recurrent subjects is that of the suffering Christ, who according to Prinzhorn, represents a superior being embodying the extremes of human weakness and superhuman strength. Christ is seen as an ambivalent figure in another sense, for 'to each Jesus belongs a Jesa'—maleness is necessarily related to femaleness. With an unrestrained frankness, Brendel frequently portrays his conception of a double being which is at once male and female. Given that man and woman are always struggling to gain the upper hand, would not the ideal solution to sexual conflict be to unite the man and the woman in one body? Brendel's fantasy (clear evidence of a 'primitive' mentality) is made tangible in a series of androgynous figures, such as *Hussar and woman*, in which the male and the female are

Karl Brendel *Christ with crown of thorns*
Prinzhorn collection, Heidelberg

Karl Brendel *Hussar and woman*
Prinzhorn collection, Heidelberg

placed back to back. Additional faces at either side mean that this double figure has four faces in all! It is further complicated by the addition of the head of the hussar's horse, and the plane he holds across his chest (a sexual connotation is likely). According to his custom, Brendel gives animal-like feet to the human figures.

Like his texts, Brendel's carvings illustrate the process of contaminatory associationism in which logical connexions are elided. The effect of incongruity is but the external effect of an interior logic at the service of an emotional complex whose power can transcend rational contradictions. One may surmise that Brendel's obsessions with Christ and the androgyne figure are related to the experience of amputation, viewed as a symbolic crucifixion or castration. The idea of 'two-in-one' may be the central impetus here. At all events Brendel's dynamic carvings are imposing evidence of the mind's ability to commit its insuperable problems to external form and, by thus externalizing them, to resolve conflict, or at least to relieve psychic tension.

Aloïse 1886–1964

On the Riviera where scented breezes murmur there every woman has dreamt of being beautiful and always adored in the blue up to the firmament the violins cast their melody. So sweet are the vows everfaithful lovers. Love it is that comes forth softly singing there on the Riviera. . . . From her virginal brow has just fallen a crown of buds of orange blossom. She prays she pardons and then falls asleep in a kiss as Empress of the roses—lying beneath the roses—of Meyerling.

These lines come from the writings of a woman who devoted much of her life to the elaboration of a personal cosmogony that, despite her alienation from the world of realizable love, constitutes a moving record of feminine desires and dreams, a record which, even though echoing the dreams of countless other women, conveys the authentic savour or pulse of original creativity. Jean Dubuffet is full of praise for the drawings of Aloïse inasmuch as they embody a vision that owes nothing to the masculine sort of art that women artists usually feel obliged to ape: 'I believe that Aloïse's tapestry with its thousand segments may be considered the one truly splendid manifestation, in painting, of the strictly feminine pulsation.'

Aloïse was born in Lausanne in 1886, into a family marked by more than one case of mental disorder. She was an intelligent if difficult child, and progressed well to her *baccalauréat*. (She took drawing lessons during these school years.) After working for a short period as a governess, she went back to her family for four years, becoming a religious fanatic and behaving in an agitated manner which was not always socially acceptable. She then left for Germany to work as a private teacher, working in Leipzig, Berlin and Potsdam, before returning to Switzerland in 1913. By now her mental disorder had become pronounced, manifesting itself in inspired religious writings and neglect of her personal appearance. Aloïse began to retreat more and more from elementary contact with people, developing a morose or rude attitude. She claimed to have a true religious calling and to be the fiancée of a parson she had once known. She wrote ardent loveletters to the German Emperor William II, whom she had once seen at a parade in Potsdam in 1913—a strange case of unhappy yet persistent love at first sight. In 1918 Aloïse had to be taken to a psychiatric clinic, where she lapsed from an agitated into a dull, autistic state. As her psychic alienation became affirmed, she was moved to the Clinique de la Rosière, where she remained to her death in 1964.

Apart from her *coup de foudre* for the German Emperor, and her association with the parson, Aloïse appears to have had an actual amorous experience at the age of fifteen, a love which may have been associated with amorous visions of Jesus Christ. Hers was thus a tremulous and dreamy inner life

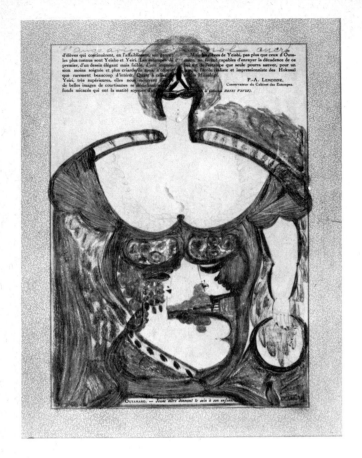

Aloïse *L'ange avion* (*The aeroplane angel*) between 1925 and 1941 drawing on a page from a magazine
Collection de l'Art Brut, Paris, courtesy Jean Dubuffet

compounded of impossible yearnings for glimpsed heroes. She evokes William II in these terms: 'his eyes like two precious diamonds whence springs a dome of stars with an ideal face wherein is revealed the universe full of splendours in the days of honeymoon where each caress of the hand in Thalia is the manna of man in the desert of pride'—an expression of impassioned admiration that veers towards self-denigration. Indeed, the initial stages of Aloïse's illness were characterized by acute feelings of inadequacy. She saw herself as 'Lulu', a girl whose rejection in love denied her any claim to personal integrity. She became a prisoner of guilt feelings, and fell into deep misery, seeing herself as 'pregnant with sulphur' and 'a wreck in the universal conflagration'.

Undoubtedly these disorders have a sexual basis. Dr Alfred Bader seems justified in pointing out the pronounced erotic content of Aloïse's drawings. For again and again she depicts women with opulent bodies and an abundance of flowing hair, attended by smart young men in military uniform. The titles of the pictures, drawn in the margins, record the associations she drew between herself and a whole retinue of famous lovers from the past: Mary Stuart, Ann Boleyn, Maria Walewska, Andromache, Ophelia. Bader proposes that we take these delirious identifications as the expression of unrequited love and unfulfilled desire, in short as a species of sexual

Aloïse *Luxembourg/en visite chez le Pape d'Avignon/Coupe fleurie Couronne étoilée/La belle Cadix derrière l'éventail* (*Luxembourg/on a visit to the Pope of Avignon/Cup with flowers Crown with stars/The beautiful Cadix behind her fan*) about 1952–4
Collection de l'Art Brut, Paris, courtesy Jean Dubuffet

Aloïse *Porter la danseuse étoile de l'opéra Paris/Napoléon III Cherbourg embrasse la reine Victoria/Dans le manteau de Bal* (*To carry the ballerina star of the opera Paris/Napoleon III Cherbourg kisses Queen Victoria/in her Ball wrap*) about 1952–4 reverse side of *Luxembourg*
Collection de l'Art Brut, Paris, courtesy Jean Dubuffet

compensation. Though banal, there is much to be said for this reading, especially as there are in Aloïse's writings passages which make a distinct call to this sort of interpretation. The following sentence occurring in the midst of a long, apparently rambling letter is surely an unequivocal evocation of an erotic experience:

> Then until I die I shall always recognize the crusader fanaticism of His Majesty because one does not know whom one has in one's arms only by means of telepathy unless it be that of his reporter Wolf always half-asleep at night one feels absolutely penetrated kissed enveloped as if one were in a bridal bed still seeing the vision of bodies which touch yours one cannot express it in any other way . . .

It is hard to resist seeing this in the light of an erotic hallucination, if not a semi-controlled sexual fantasy. Yet Mme Jacqueline Porret-Forel (who knew Aloïse for about twenty years) contends that the problem is far more complex. In her view, Aloïse had a horror of men, and chose as her imaginary lovers only those male figures who, by virtue of their inaccessibility, would not represent a danger to her virginity. She goes so far as to speak of Aloïse's 'revenge on man' as expressed through the sphinx-like figure with breasts but no lower body who bears a sword to defend the woman against male attacks. Mme Porret-Forel considers the extravagant depiction of women in Aloïse's pictures as against the neutral rendering of the male figures as a further index of a frigid attitude towards love. I find it hard to accept this explanation: the more so since Aloïse herself has been quoted as speaking of herself as an old maid in terms that reveal not so much a horror of sex as a regret for her own lost chances: 'I've remained a bit on the shelf, a bit Catholic, that's why I'd like the other ladies to do the opposite, and amuse themselves.'

After her personality collapse, Aloïse at first saw herself as 'black earth, a scarecrow for sparrows'. Then, bit by bit, she began to reconstruct her ruined world. Her schizophrenic thinking was able to put right her humiliation and restore her integrity, her sacrifice becoming the basis of a glorious reincarnation as a kind of feminine principle informing the whole cosmos. Lulu, the isolated martyr, turned into a being of cosmic power, identifying herself with the earth seen now as the firm support for her protean expansion: 'this matter, this mud become in their bodies a Saturn or saturated with stars'—base matter is transmuted in quasi-alchemical fashion into a radiant centre of energy. Now creator of her own world, Aloïse 'gives birth' to all things; she is a Madonna and a goddess, she becomes a star, a flower, the statue of Liberty, shining gold. Total integration is realized thanks to the

notion of the 'solar ricochet', a process whereby Aloïse, in her incarnation as the earth, reflects the light of the divine sun, casting it forth to illuminate and so 'create' the stars, the moon, and the rest of her shining cosmos. This mechanism allows her to participate in the being of any and every object or person in the system: she becomes omnipresent, omnipotent, sharing in the transfigured life of all things. The Catholic notion of the Trinity, the three-in-one that affirms unity within separateness, is developed into the idea of 'alternative consubstantiality', which denotes Aloïse's capacity to change places with any of her creatures and move successively through all states and levels of her imagined realm. Thanks to this concept, she can attain a sense of unity within her world of vacillating images. She can be Cleopatra, Marie de Médicis, Marie-Antoinette, Joséphine, la belle Otéro; equally she can participate in the being of the lovers that complete the dream of union: Jupiter, Romeo, François I, Napoleon, Chopin, even Luther and Pope Pius XII; and again, she can partake of the attributes and settings that go to make up the rest of the pictures: flowers, pearls, tiaras, thrones, gardens, palaces. Throughout this system, Aloïse has the freedom to pass where she wishes. Her projected world is totally hers.

Ultimately Aloïse was aiming at what she calls, obscurely, the 'incarnation of the picture', which phrase apparently denotes the eventual actualization of the perfect cosmos—a transportation of the schizophrenic world-picture on to the plane of actuality, a literal realization of what is in fact only fantasy —albeit grandiose and magnificent fantasy. The stages of her psychic process are thus: alienation, reconstruction and attempted reintegration. The creation of an alternative world corresponds to Aloïse's attempt to remould her damaged personality; condemned in fact to elaborate a purely disembodied universe, she nonetheless managed to create a support for her personality so coherent in its construction that towards the end of her life she could entertain the idea of its being literally capable of life. Her system was indeed coherent, vital, endlessly creative. It nourished her absolutely. But in the last analysis, the concretization of her cosmos could only be attained through the long and rich production of her art.

Aloïse had creative capacities in more than one field. She had a good singing voice, and would often sit by the clinic window in the evening and go through a repertoire of operatic arias. Her love of opera is apparent from the references to composers that recur in her writings or the titles of her drawings. Aloïse composed a number of texts of considerable poetic appeal, combining religious vocabulary, echoes of Swiss folk song and reminiscences of theatrical or historical personages with bursts of wholly original inspiration. The lack of punctuation in these writings suggests a constant flow of fertile ideas; according to Mme Porret-Forel, the associations of thought were not arbitrary but highly meaningful to Aloïse. During her long stay at La Rosière, Aloïse became famous for the extreme care and efficiency which she devoted to the task of ironing, always completing each day's allotted pile before turning to her pencils. Something of this thoroughness and zeal comes across in the drawings. In early years, Aloïse used old scraps of paper, including parcel wrappings with stamps stuck on; even when she had access to higher quality material, she would often take a distinct pleasure in using crumpled sheets of coarse paper, which she would carefully smooth out before setting to work. She used cheap coloured pencils with a wax base, which rendered a shiny surface if rubbed over; sometimes in the fever of creation she would use saliva to help distribute the colours over a large area. In her early days at the clinic, she drew in secret, but later grew so absorbed by her work that she no longer noticed if anyone was watching. It was observed that she would first draw the outlines of her figures, then at once put in the blue ovals that represent the eyes. Then, working at top speed and probably without worrying very much which pencil she picked up next, she would fill in the colours over the whole surface of the drawing. A single impulse seems to reverberate across the entire picture; the impression of harmony deriving from what Dubuffet calls the 'uniform vehemence' of her pencilling. The drawings are composed without regard for any conventions of perspective, proportion or colouring. Sections of one design sometimes overlap on to a fresh piece of paper, many compositions being made up of several different sheets sewn together and attaining in some cases a length of several yards. The general impression is of an endlessly buoyant epic creation in which, as in the writings, punctuation (division into distinct components) has no place: the pictures form one continuous fresco of epic proportions.

The décor is usually theatrical, there being frequent details that refer directly to the theatre: curtains, balconies, the orchestra. The trappings or 'scenery' are of a typically feminine type: bouquets of roses, gondolas, nuptial decorations, and the like. The central figure in Aloïse's drawings is always a woman of queenly bearing, dressed in ermine or clinging brocade, often with a crown upon her magnificent head of blonde or red hair. Her dress opens to reveal a proud expanse of bosom, the breasts swelling forth like buds about to flower. Occasionally the woman is naked, and is clearly meant to incarnate the highest blossoming of female beauty. The fecund attribute of the flower is never lacking: flowers surround her, pour from her, are confused with her. In this heady ambience of femininity, the male consort cuts a comparatively insignificant figure—but I would argue that he is not for all that irremediably marked down as inferior to the woman, though Mme Porret-Forel insists that he becomes practically

invisible. The man's clothing is admittedly not very colourful, but he is always smart, and his face looks as if it were intended to render an ideal of male beauty. Mme Porret-Forel observes that the relationship between female and male became most intimate only after about 1950, up to which point Aloïse had been unable to overcome her inhibitions. Subsequently her drawings depicted quite ardent embraces in which the lovers' lips press together almost to compose a single face.

The eyes of all the figures drawn by Aloïse are represented invariably by blue (or occasionally violet or green) almond or oval shapes. These are

168

Aloïse *Matador qui fuit d'Orient toute la terre adorée/couchés dans l'orchidées les tabuutes (Matador fleeing from the East all the adored earth/they lie amid tabu orchids)* detail from *Dancing* 1952
Collection de l'Art Brut, Paris, courtesy Jean Dubuffet

not a representation of a mask, as might be thought (masks are supposedly characteristic of the drawings of schizophrenics) but rather of eyes without pupils. It is as though the lack of pupils expresses a refusal to admit externals, and a corresponding preference for the superior colours of interior vision. Aloïse herself once suggested that the ovals represent glasses: 'They were embarrassed when it came to kissing, so they wear glasses.' Bader sees this as indicating a form of magical protection against the strictures of external reality, an invitation to the wearer of the glasses to respond freely to forbidden passion. Mme Porret-Forel's complementary interpretation is that the blue eyes denote blindness (Aloïse herself began to lose her sight in her old age): 'The eye blinded with blue allows the person to partake of the mythical and theatrical world which she created and which is a kind of half-way point from which the incarnate world can be regained. Lack of sight permits her characters to experience all that she herself was denied.'

Aloïse's is indeed a theatrical creation, a mythology whose *raison d'être* ultimately lies in its cultivation of the unreal rather than in any collusion with reality. Above all she loved situations that were not subject to everyday laws: her scenes are operatic or fairy-tale tableaux almost completely divorced from her normal experience of life in the clinic. Dubuffet contends that the camellias, roses and water-lilies that are crammed into the drawings play a purely metaphorical rôle. Along with the resplendent breasts, hair and jewelry of Aloïse's woman, they are the figures of a rhetoric that has no content. Hence his assertion that the whole pantomime has no physical significance at all, a performance that remains within strictly conceptual limits being devoid of any literal weight. The hypothesis is strengthened when one notes how Aloïse entirely discarded any ability she may have acquired to draw 'correctly' and deformed her subjects so as to make of them purely mental products. The manipulation of forms unrelated to the actual world would in this sense offer a rigorous example of autistic creation that in conjuring up an alternative reality deliberately avoids attributing to it the palpability that is such an elementary quality of normal sensory experience—the invented world has no solidity, it is cerebral, detached. This speaks for the completeness and the intellectual purity of Aloïse's work. For my own part, I cannot but respond to the awakening feeling of erotic plenitude that is conveyed not only by the later drawings; an outsider's reaction of this sort might be envisaged as in some way the realization of Aloïse's ideal of the 'incarnation of the picture', and perhaps the breaking of a taboo—the transposition of metaphor on to the plane of the concrete.

See also illustrations pages 28, 133.

Simon Rodia 1879–

Watts is a sprawling suburb of Los Angeles, a drab and dusty accumulation of one-storey houses and vacant lots. Above East 107 Street, a short street that runs between two railroad tracks, three tall spires soar upwards, the highest rising to something like one hundred feet. They are skeletal structures formed by interlinked rings that create a dense, fantastic tracery. Several smaller spires accompany them, all being incrusted with a gaily coloured mosaic of broken china, glass and shells. Around the triangular lot runs a six-foot scalloped wall. From inside, the towers are seen to be connected by overhead arches and spokes; stalagmites, fountains, birdbaths, loggias and benches rise out of a floor of slabs of red, brown and green cement marked with flower- and heart-shaped patterns. The inside wall and all other available surfaces are covered in sea-shells, green 7-Up bottles, broken cups and the like, or with cement that bears the impressions made by hammers, pliers, screwdrivers, scrap ironwork, corncobs, cookie moulds, sewing-machine parts, and the rosette-shaped handle of an old tap. The surrounding wall is high enough to dismiss the outer world from one's consciousness; the array of disparate parts takes on an exhilarating coherence and forms a harmonious space set apart, a closed garden which nourishes the sense of wonderment and refuses the ordinariness of its suburban context.

The creator of the Watts Towers is an uneducated Italian workman, Simon Rodia, who was taken to the United States in about 1888, while still a child. After doing jobs as a logger, miner and construction worker, he went to Los Angeles to work as a tile-setter and telephone repair-man, buying a house in Watts. He was a simple unschooled man, whose leisure time was spent reading odd volumes of an old *Encyclopaedia Britannica*, from which he derived an admiration for figures such as Alexander the Great, Julius Caesar, and Buffalo Bill. It is possible that these heroes inspired him to seek a way to leave his own mark in life or, as he once put it, 'to do something big'. In 1921 he began to build in his garden, having, so he claimed, acquired a building permit issued by the state capital Sacramento, Los Angeles having refused. Without plans, without machinery, without scaffolding, Rodia set to work, erecting steel rods, meshing wire round them, and adding waterproof cement to form a powerful armature. First he constructed a twenty-five foot tower of interconnected hoops; then he started again at the bottom and built another structure around the first, carrying the tower up twenty feet higher, and so on. The hoops were close enough together for him to climb up without a ladder, with a window-washer's belt for safety and a bucket of cement. Rodia had no assistance. 'I was a poor man', he is quoted as saying. 'Had to do a little at a time. Nobody helped me. I think if I hire a man he don't know what to

Simon Rodia The Watts Towers

do. A million times I don't know what to do myself.' Apart from the cement, Rodia bought none of his materials and relied on what he could pick up from the neighbourhood. He would go for walks at night with an empty cement sack on his shoulder, gathering bottles and other bits and pieces; the railroad gave him some rusty old rails, and at weekends he would take the tram to Long Beach and gather shells. For thirty-three years he carried on his work, and then, in 1954, before the garden was properly finished, he abruptly called a halt, signed his property away to a neighbour and disappeared. For years the property lay uncared for, vandals threw stones at the towers, and parts of the mosaic were smashed. (A rumour had it that money was hidden behind the plates in the wall.) In 1955 the house burned down, and thereafter the garden turned more and more into a rubbish dump. However, by 1959 a number of people had become interested in the Towers and were resolved to preserve them, despite a threat by the city to demolish what it saw as illegal and dangerous structures. After a long-drawn dispute the committee set up to defend the Towers agreed to an engineering test to ascertain whether they were safe or not. When subjected to strain equivalent to a 70 m.p.h. wind, the reinforced concrete did not budge, and the city's case was lost. Since then the garden has been cleaned up, and declared a Culture Heritage Monument.

But are the Watts Towers a 'cultural' work in the sense of a contribution to a felt tradition? The engineering test at least assures their endurance, but the fact that the garden has been opened to the public is no guarantee that the work really 'belongs' to a collective heritage. It may be doubted whether the varied reactions that people have are of any relevance to the original intention that underlay the creation of the Towers. Some visitors have said that the triangular slip of land with its three 'masts' feels like a ship. Others are attentive to the rumour that Rodia's wife lies buried underneath the tallest tower, and like to imagine that the Towers are a monument to a woman's memory. Yet others have wanted to see the Towers as a tribute to California, Rodia's new homeland, though Rodia's work could just as well be envisaged as a violent reaction against it, or at least to the immediate area of Watts. It might be held that the Towers are a challenge to triviality and ugliness, a 'something big' that is not mimetic of American bigness, but a brilliant alternative to it in the way it exploits the very things that America discards. The only inscriptions to be found are the Spanish words 'Nuestro Pueblo', repeated several times, notably on the main gate and the principal tower. The expression has been variously construed as 'Our Town' or 'Our People', and as a reminiscence of the original name of the city, El Pueblo Nuestra Señora la Reina de Los Angeles de Porciuncula. Yet rather than reinforce the sense of its kinship with that city, the naming of the garden in this way could equally draw attention to its separateness—it is *Our* Town as against *Their* Town. That is, the name may imply a gesture of dissociation, of solitary withdrawal. The high walls around the lot confirm its separatist autonomy: the place could be defended like a fort!

As for Rodia himself, he was finally traced by members of the Towers Committee, who found him living in a bedsitter in Martinez, three hundred-odd miles to the north. But they were unable to get anything much out of him by way of a statement of intention. The old man preferred to discuss politics. When pressed to explain the name Nuestro Pueblo, he replied evasively that it means 'lot-sa things, lot-sa things'. Why had he left Watts? The only satisfactory reason that emerged was that he was tired of being harrassed by vandals. It was noted that he never mentioned having finished the work. Though courteous, Rodia at all times remained indifferent to the enthusiasm of his admirers, and the one striking statement he made was that he was not interested in going back to see his work: 'Don't you understand? It's the end; there's nothing there.' Our curiosity about the Towers seems dilettantish in the face of such perfect renunciation.

Audrey 1949–

Educated in the grammar section of an English comprehensive school, Audrey showed above average intelligence, though she completed only one 'o'-level examination. She showed no interest in Art as taught in class, and gave up the subject early, convinced that she had no artistic ability. After leaving school at the age of sixteen, she worked for a few years as a typist until the onset of schizophrenia, characterized in particular by auditory hallucinations. Abusive voices whisper to her that she is of no use to anyone, that she is worth nothing. She imagines her head is growing bigger and bigger. What Prinzhorn termed the 'mobilization of a latent creative urge' was the reaction to the schizophrenic collapse, Audrey's compulsive doodling being thus a defence mechanism against the persecutions of her 'horrible monsters'. Rapidly executed in blue and green felt-tip pens on the drawing pad she carries around at all times, her drawings depict menacing eyes and the feelers of repulsive insects. The process of exorcism is carried out with cleanliness and control, and it is hard to

Audrey Drawing 1971
Courtesy Mrs J. Spurgeon

reconcile an impression of decorative poise with the knowledge that these are drawings of horror. Equally ambivalent is Audrey's attitude to her work, about which she seems possessive while at the same time desirous to be rid of it. At present she is receiving drug treatment at intervals which correspond to her creative spells, the latter being most intense at the times when the effects of the drug are minimal. It seems probable that she will soon go into a psychiatric hospital.

Emmanuel 1908–65

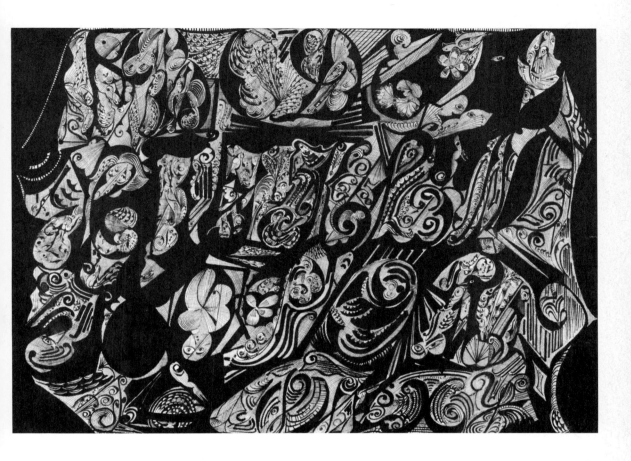

Emmanuel drawing no. 2, 1959
Collection de l'Art Brut, Paris, courtesy Jean Dubuffet

Of pure Breton stock, Emmanuel was born of working-class parents at
Guingamp in 1908. As the result of a fall as a baby, he spent his childhood
as an invalid, using crutches until the age of ten. His father having died
at the end of the war, Emmanuel was brought up in Brest by his mother
and sister in a markedly feminine atmosphere, spending long evenings
with them doing lacework and making artificial flowers. This undoubtedly
instilled in him a love of embroidery and intricate decoration. At one
point in his schooling, he took voluntary drawing lessons, but did not take
this interest any further. When he left school at seventeen he became a

Emmanuel *The siren of the seas* (no. 26) 1963
Collection de l'Art Brut, Paris, courtesy Jean Dubuffet

book-keeper. An early marriage led to a divorce, and he went back to
live with his mother in Brest; in 1936 he married again and had four children.
After the war, Emmanuel began drinking heavily and had violent quarrels
with his wife. The disruptive effects of alcoholism were aggravated by various
ailments and accidents. In 1953 he had to undergo treatment at a psychiatric
hospital in Quimper, manifesting delirious mania in connection with
chronic alcoholism. Though this stay was a short one, he had to return to
the hospital in 1958 for a period lasting eight years. Classified as paraphrenic,
Emmanuel was excitable and imaginative, and given to fantastic fabrications on religious subjects. When encouraged to frequent the art therapy
centre, Emmanuel, at the age of fifty, began to draw for the first time since
childhood. He soon refused all guidance, and started to produce his own
original work, at first doing some figurative paintings, then turning to black
inks in an evident attempt to work out a truly inventive idiom. His experiments were apparently inspired by the baroque adornments on the
lettering at the head of some account-books; indeed some of his pictures
comprise alphabets worked up into complicated mosaics. The method was

to explore the possibilities inherent in the given form, a letter such as s prompting sometimes a fish, sometimes a bird: without any preconceived notion of where he was going, Emmanuel added detail upon detail until he had built up the complete picture. This calligraphic elaboration was carried out with patient attention and with a whole range of instruments—pens, brushes, hair, fingers, etc. He developed techniques of diluting the inks, and introducing coloured areas of gouache. His images are a persuasive mixture of familiar and unfamiliar creatures: pigeons and snails coexist with dragons and mermaids, and all are bound together in a taut web of interwoven threads. Of his pictures Emmanuel commented that one could find in them 'various motifs in the Chinese style merging into arabesques which give rise to burlesque caricatures which it is rather difficult to describe precisely. The imagination alone can draw out various subjects. With the details I give, it is obviously open to any other person to use his imagination and see other subjects than those I point out.' While it is crucial to bear in mind this entirely 'open' situation as regards interpretation, it is worth quoting Emmanuel's own description of the picture *The siren of the seas*:

> The mermaid is at the bottom left in the form of an s, her tail reaching across to the back of the Chinese lady who stands erect, draped with a butterfly. The mermaid is also represented by a woman whose head is caught inside a flower; round her neck is a cray-fish, lower down is a butterfly on her dress which goes down to the bottom with embroidery motifs. Above are a bird and a sun, below a saw-bird, in the middle the Moon; in the sail that is used as a fishing-net are two fish.

Complex to the point of polyvalence, the pictures of Emmanuel remain fresh and gay, and are entirely without morbidity. In 1964, he was discharged from hospital and, since his wife refused to see him, took a small room in Brest on his own. Though he did not manage to produce any further pictures before his sudden death in 1965, he had in mind to execute a series using sea-weed soaked in ink. He hoped to overcome the difficulties he had in walking by learning to ride a bicycle, and so get to the beach to collect his materials.

See also illustration page 48.

3 Aberrant paths

The philistine habit of using the concept 'sick' to minimize
and disparage draws a veil across a reality which we
are by no means in a position to interpret, indeed whose
formulation still gives us much trouble, presumably
because we are entangled in restricted categories of
appreciation and in a framework of ideas which still
binds us, whilst we feel it loosening in favour of one
which is more extensive, more free, more mobile.

Karl Jaspers *Strindberg und van Gogh* 1922

An alternative art exists. It need not be geographically remote, nor need it have a single location. It crops up in all the places where Art is considered to have no place. In its brutal purity, it displays no pleasant surface beauty, but exposes smudges and flaws that are too unrefined to pass through the filtering baleen of the Whale of Good Taste. Raw creation is hard to stomach: it is unfamiliar, uncanny, even savage and coarse. But it is never degenerate or watered-down. For creation that is truly inventive, that genuinely stimulates passion, will be creation springing directly from the original sources of emotion and not something tapped from the cultural reservoir. As fully proof liquor, art brut is healthy and invigorating—any vertigo it introduces is salutary! Festive or tragic, cerebral or feverish, gratuitous or implacable, it must always be *different* for the same reason that individuals are always different. Once we step inside the confines of an autistic sensibility, we are faced with a unique and incisive truth that casts its distinct spell. Which way do we jump when confronted with art that makes so few concessions? Here we may appreciate the terrorist function of aberrant creation: for the art that thrusts us into emotional and in-tellectual situations beyond our normal grasp, serving us explanations of reality—our reality?—in a language that is unprecedented and a-historical, is an art of tonic doubt that will threaten the reliability of our readymade postures and expose the wobbly props of our petrified heritage.

If we are reading this book, we cannot call ourselves uncultured; hence we cannot hope just by shrugging our shoulders to relinquish the apparatus of thought and the reflexes of taste that have governed us for so long. Yet the high voltage of alienated creativity can sometimes release flashes sufficient to blind us momentarily to the dictates graven by our elders, producing an instant of intuitive *décervelage* in which we are violently aware of the savage within us. The intuition of our own primitivism can encourage us to nourish the individuality we tend to hide and find our authentic register.

If art brut is not a static place on the map, it can be a direction. Its rare light beckons towards an impossible horizon where the most intensely human merges into the abhuman. Towards this pole of utter self-sufficiency the solitary creator is drawn, if need be loosing all ties with the collectivity. If we try to follow the same aberrant paths with only our inadequate com-pass of aesthetic ideas or our reverential memories of established master-pieces, we are likely to feel lost. Even to speak of 'art' is to drag along a word that loses its relevance. The alternative art is resistant to labels, being created by individuals who have recognized that what counts is not produce but process, and for whom the mobility of thought or deed is more important than its apparent target.

Totally alien, the new art (an art that has always been) proliferates quietly round the outskirts of the cultural city. The present survey of what this art can offer, being only provisional and partial, thus ends not with the complacent humming emitted by art-books that fit snug next to what has gone before, but with the busy, uneven clattering made by the nameless creators presently engaged in erecting alternative realities, sounds which—such is the present state of our sensibility—are yet too disparate for us to apprehend as a single message. Whether or not the time will ever come when those untutored hands will fashion a Trojan Horse, the siege of the cultural city is underway.

Bibliography

1 Art brut

L'Art Brut   Publications de la Compagnie de l'Art Brut, nos. 1–8, Paris 1964–6. (Studies on the most important artists in the Art Brut collection. Most are by Jean Dubuffet, and are reprinted in *Prospectus* 1.)

L'Art Brut   catalogue of the exhibition in the Musée des Arts décoratifs, Paris 1967

Catalogue de la collection de l'Art Brut   Paris 1971

Dubuffet, Jean   'L'Art brut préféré aux arts culturels' 1949; 'Honneur aux valeurs sauvages' 1951; 'Place à l'incivisme' 1967; all in *Prospectus et tous écrits suivants* I and II Paris 1967 (Dubuffet's collected writings) *Asphyxiante culture*, Paris 1968

Pierre, José   'D'une autre prise de la Bastille', *L'Archibras* no. 2, Paris 1967

Pluchart, François   'Saveur et authenticité de l'Art brut', *Flammes et fumées*, Paris 1967

2 Madness and art

Bader, Alfred, Hans Steck, Georg Schmidt, Jean Cocteau: *Insania pingens— Petits maîtres de la folie* Lausanne 1961 (*Though this be madness* London 1963)

Bildnerei der Geisteskranken, Art Brut, Insania pingens   catalogue of an exhibition at the Kunsthalle, Bern 1963

Bobon, Jean   *Psychopathologie de l'expression* Paris 1962

Breton, André   'L'Art des fous, la clé des champs', *La Clé des champs* Paris 1953

Crowcroft, Andrew   *The Psychotic—Understanding Madness* Harmondsworth 1967

Delay, Jean   *Expressions plastiques de la folie*, Paris 1956

Foucault, Michel   *Histoire de la folie* Paris 1961 (*Madness and civilization* London 1967)

Gentis, Roger   *Les Murs de l'asile* Paris 1971

Imaginäre Welten—Gestalteter Wahn   catalogue of an exhibition of schizophrenic art, Hanover 1970

Jakab, Irène   *Dessins et peintures des aliénés* Budapest 1956

Jaspers, Karl   *Strindberg und van Gogh* Berlin 1922

Kris, Ernst *Psychoanalytic Explorations in Art* New York 1952

Laing, Ronald D. *The Divided Self* London 1960

Lo Duca 'L'Art, les fous et les naïfs', introduction to Anatole Jakovsky, *Eros du dimanche* Paris 1964

Lombroso, Cesare *Genio e follia* Turin 1882

Navratil, Leo *Schizophrenie und Kunst* Munich 1965
  Schizophrenie und Sprache Munich 1966
  'Psychose und Kreativität', *Hippokrates* no. 15, 1969
  'Pareidolien', catalogue of an exhibition of work by Navratil's patients, Vienna 1970
  a + b leuchten im Klee—Psychopathologische Texte, Munich 1971

Plokker, J. H. *Artistic self-expression in mental disease: the shattered image of schizophrenics*, London and The Hague 1964

Prinzhorn, Hans *Bildnerei der Geisteskranken*, Berlin 1922. (2nd edition 1923; reprinted 1968. First English version *Artistry of the Mentally Ill*, Berlin and New York 1971)

Psychopathologie de l'expression (collection of studies on psychopathology and figurative expression published regularly for the psychiatric profession in French, German and English by Sandoz AG, Paris and Basle)

Rainer, Arnulf 'Schön und Wahn', *Jahrbuch Protokolle* Vienna 1967
  'Katatonenkunst', *Manuskripte* Graz 1969
  'Euthanasie der Kunst', *Neues Forum* Vienna 1969
  'Die 13. Muse oder Wahnsinn eine Kunstart' *Jahrbuch Protokolle* Vienna 1970

Rave-Schwank, Maria, Jan M. Broekman, Wolfgang Rothe *Bildnerei der Geisteskranken aus der Prinzhorn-Sammlung* catalogue of the first public exhibition of works from the Prinzhorn collection, Heidelberg 1967

Reitmann, Francis *Psychotic Art* London 1950

Réja, Marcel *L'Art chez les fous*, Paris 1905

Rennert, Helmut *Die Merkmale schizophrener Bildnerei*, Jena 1962

Schilder, Paul *Wahn und Erkenntnis—eine psychopathologische Studie*, Berlin 1918

Spiessbach, Erich *Wahnsinn, Ironie und tiefere Bedeutung*, Leverkusen 1970

Vinchon, Jean *L'Art et la folie*, 2nd edition, Paris 1950

Volmat, Robert *L'Art psychopathologique*, Paris 1956. (Based on the international exhibition of the First World Psychiatry Congress, Paris 1950. Documents over 320 cases and contains exhaustive bibliography.)

3 General material

Bataille, Georges   'L'Art primitif', *Documents* Paris 1930

Bihalji-Merin, Oto   *Das naive Bild der Welt* Cologne 1959
Modern Primitives London 1971

Blasdel, Gregg N.   'The Grass-Roots Artist', *Art in America* September-October 1968

Boas, Franz   *Primitive Art* 1927 (new edition, New York 1955)

Breton, André   'Le Message automatique', *Minotaure* no. 3/4, Paris 1933
'Autodidactes dits naïfs' (1942) in *Le Surréalisme et la peinture* new edition Paris 1965

Caillois, Roger   'Première approche', *Au coeur du fantastique* Paris 1965
'Les traces', *Cases d'un échiquier* Paris 1970

Conrad, Ulrich and Hans Sperlich   *Fantastic Architecture* London 1963

Jean Dubuffet   catalogue of an exhibition of paintings by Dubuffet at the Tate Gallery, London 1966
'Dubuffet—culture et subversion', *L'Arc* no. 35 Paris 1968

Ehrenzweig, Anton   *The Hidden Order of Art* London 1967

Ehrmann, Gilles   *Les Inspirés et leurs demeures*, Paris 1962

Hirn, Yrjö   *The Origins of Art*, London 1900

Hocke, Gustav René   *Die Welt als Labyrinth—Manier und Manie in der europäischen Kunst*, Hamburg 1963

Jakovsky, Anatole   *Les Peintres naïfs*, Paris 1956
Dämonen und Wunder, Cologne 1963

Jasmand, Bernhard and Otto Kallir   *Sonntagsmaler*, Berlin 1956

Kelemen, Boris   *La Peinture naïve yougoslave*, Zagreb 1969

Kupka, Karel   *Un Art à l'état brut*, Lausanne 1962 (*Dawn of Art*, London/Sydney 1965)

Luquet, G. H.   *Le Dessin enfantin*, Paris 1935

Monnerot, Jules   'Primitifs' in *La Poésie moderne et le sacré*, Paris 1945

Prinzhorn, Hans   *Bildnerei der Gefangenen*, Berlin 1926

Toller, Jane   *Prisoners-of-war Work 1756–1815*, Cambridge 1965

Uhde, Wilhelm   *Fünf primitive Meister*, Zürich 1947

Wingert, Paul S.   *Primitive Art—its traditions and styles*, New York 1962

4 Specific studies

Aloïse

'Ecrits d'Aloïse', *L'Art Brut* no. 7, 1966

Bader, Alfred   'La vie et l'oeuvre d'Aloyse', *Insania Pingens—Petits maîtres de la folie* 1961

Dubuffet, Jean   'Haut Art d'Aloïse', *L'Art Brut* no. 7

Porret-Forel, Jacqueline   'Aloïse et son théâtre', *L'Art Brut* no. 7

Karl Brendel

Prinzhorn, Hans   *Bildnerei der Geisteskranken* 1922

Gaston Chaissac

Chaissac, Gaston   *Hippobosque au bocage* Paris 1949
   'Gaston Chaissac', *Suites* no. 28 Geneva May 1970

Dubuffet, Jean   'Peintures et dessins de Gaston Chaissac', *Prospectus* II, 1967

Jakovsky, Anatole   *Gaston Chaissac—l'homme orchestre* Paris 1952

Péret, Benjamin   'Ici l'on métamorphose . . .', G. Ehrmann *Les Inspirés et leurs demeures* 1962

Ferdinand Cheval

Borne, Alain   *Le Facteur Cheval* Forcalquier 1969

Brunius, Jacques   'Le Palais idéal', *Architectural Review*, London October 1936

Ehrmann, Gilles   'Le Facteur Ferdinand Cheval à Hauterives', *Les Inspirés et leurs demeures* 1962

Guégen, Pierre   'Architecture et sculpture naïves—le palais du Facteur Cheval à Hauterives', *Aujourd'hui*, Paris June 1956

Jakovsky, Anatole   'Der ideale Palast des Briefträgers Cheval', *Dämonen und Wunder* 1963

Jean, André   *Le Palais idéal du Facteur Cheval à Hauterives Drôme* Grenoble 1952

Miskin, Lionel   'The Sculpture of the Facteur Cheval at the Palais idéal of Hauterives', *Stand* 8 no. 3, 1966–7

Joseph Crépin

Bounoure, Vincent   'Crépin, un grand irrégulier de la peinture', *Nord-Magazine* no. 5, February 1970

Breton, André 'Joseph Crépin' (1954) *Le Surréalisme et la peinture* 1965

Dubuffet, Jean 'Joseph Crépin', *L'Art Brut* no. 5, 1965

Jules Dou

Bader, Alfred 'La vie et l'oeuvre de Jules', *Insania pingens—Petits maîtres de la folie* 1961

Gaston Duf

Dubuffet, Jean 'Gaston le zoologue' in *L'Art Brut* no. 5, 1965

Bernard, P. and Bobon, J. 'Le Rînhâûzhâîrhhâûsês, néomorphisme compensatoire chez un paraphrène débile', *Acta Neurologica et Psychiatrica Belgica* January 1964

Emmanuel

Dubuffet, Jean 'Emmanuel le calligraphe', *L'Art Brut* no. 4, 1965

Adolphe-Julien Fouéré

Brebion, H. *La Légende des Rochers sculptés de Rothéneuf* Mâcon 1968

Ehrmann, Gilles 'Adolphe-Julien Fouéré l'ermite de Rothéneuf', *Les Inspirés et leurs demeures* 1962

Jakovsky, Anatole 'Die Felsskulpturen von Rotheneuf', *Dämonen und Wunder*, 1963

Madge Gill

Interview in *Prediction* London 1937

Interview in *Psychic News* London 1942

Gill, Laurence E. 'Myrninerest the Spheres', broadsheet issued March 1926

Green, James 'Inspired Art—the drawings of Madge Gill', in catalogue of an exhibition at East Ham Town Hall, 1969

Spencer, Charles 'Madge Gill—the guided hand', in catalogue of an exhibition at Grosvenor Gallery, London 1968

Guillaume

Dequeker, Jean *Monographie d'un psychopathe dessinateur. Etude de son style* Rodez 1948

Dubuffet, Jean 'Guillaume', *L'Art Brut* no. 4, 1965

Raymond Isidore

Ehrmann, Gilles 'Raymond Isidore employé à l'entretien du cimetière de Chartres', *Les Inspirés et leurs demeures* 1962

Jakovsky, Anatole 'Raymond Isidore', *Dämonen und Wunder* 1963

August Klotz

Prinzhorn, Hans *Bildnerei der Geisteskranken* 1922

Johann Knüpfer

Prinzhorn, Hans *Bildnerei der Geisteskranken* 1922

Augustin Lesage

Dubuffet, Jean 'Le Mineur Lesage', *L'Art Brut* no. 3, 1965 (contains extracts from report by Dr E. Osty)

Pascal Maisonneuve

Edelmann, Michèle 'Les Coquilles de Maisonneuve', *L'Art Brut* no. 3, 1965

Peter Moog

Prinzhorn, Hans *Bildnerei der Geisteskranken* 1922

Heinrich Anton Müller

Dubuffet, Jean 'Heinrich Anton M.', *L'Art Brut* no. 1, 1964

August Neter

Prinzhorn, Hans *Bildnerei der Geisteskranken* 1922

Palanc

Dubuffet, Jean 'Palanc l'écrituriste', *L'Art Brut* no. 1, 1964

Laure Pigeon

Dubuffet, Jean 'La double vie de Laure', *L'Art Brut* no. 6, 1966

Simon Rodia

Jakovsky, Anatole 'Die Türme von Watts', *Dämonen und Wunder* 1963

Langsner, Jules 'Sam of Watts', *Arts and Architecture* July 1951

Seitz, William C. *The Art of Assemblage* New York 1961

Silvy, Maurice 'Les Tours de Watts de Sam Rodillo à Los Angeles' *Aujourd'hui* no. 8 June 1956

Trillin, Calvin 'A Reporter at Large—I know I want to do something', *New Yorker* New York May 1965

The Watts Towers booklet issued by Committee for Simon Rodia's Towers in Watts

Clarence Schmidt

Kaprow, Allen *Assemblage, Environments and Happenings* New York n.d.

Friedrich Schröder-Sonnenstern

Laszlo, Carl *Schroeder-Sonnenstern* (with an autobiography by the artist) Basle 1962

Scottie Wilson

Dubuffet, Jean 'Scottie Wilson', *L'Art Brut* no. 4, 1965 (contains texts by V. Musgrave and A. De Maine)

Levy, Mervyn 'Scottie Wilson's Kingdom in Kilburn', *Studio* no. 830 London, June 1962
Scottie Wilson London 1966

Adolf Wölfli

Adolf Wölfli catalogue of an exhibition of his works from a private collection at the Kupferstichkabinett, Basle 1971

Morgenthaler, Walter *Ein Geisteskranker als Künstler* Bern 1921 (translated by Henri-Pol Bouché under the title *Adolf Wölfli* for *L'Art Brut* no. 2, 1964, with a preface 'Nomenclatures insurrectionnelles')

Von Ries, Julius *Uber das dämonisch-sinnliche und den Ursprung der ornamentalen Kunst des Geisteskranken Adolf Wölfli* Bern 1946

Spoerri, Theodor 'L'Armoire d'Adolf Wölfli', *Le Surréalisme, même* no. 4, spring 1958
Die Bilderwelt Adolf Wölflis Basle 1964

Bogosav Živković

Bihalji-Merin, Oto *Bogosav Živković—the world of a primitive sculptor* London 1962

Dubuffet, Jean 'Pièces d'arbre historiées de Bogosav Živković', *L'Art Brut* no. 8, 1966

Acknowledgements

Acknowledgement of the sources of illustrations is made against each item as it appears. I would particularly like to express my gratitude to Jean Dubuffet for permission to reproduce a great deal of material from the Collection de l'Art Brut, and to Slavko Kopac and Mme G. Riberolles for showing me round the collection and helping me with my choice of photos; to Professor W. von Baeyer for permission to reproduce material from the Prinzhorn collection in Heidelberg; to Dr D. L. Davies for permission to reproduce material from the Guttmann-Maclay collection; to Dr Leo Navratil, Dr Alfred Bader, Dr Christian Peter Rode, Arnulf Rainer, and Sandoz AG for providing me with very useful documents; to Jean Benoit, Micheline Bounoure, Anatole Jakovsky, Maurice Olsen, José Pierre, Mme N. Poirson, Dr Wolfgang Rothe and Mr Beryl Sokoloff for offering me helpful suggestions as well as photographic material; to Professor Th. Spoerri for allowing me access to Wölfli drawings from the Waldau collection; to Mrs S. Estorick for letting me consult material by Madge Gill at the Grosvenor Gallery, London, and to Mr James Green for showing me the Madge Gill collection in the Newham (London) Library; to Miss Vera Ling and Mrs H. Gatenby for providing me with much important information about Madge Gill, and to Mrs J. Spurgeon for information about Audrey; to Jim Styles, Mrs Alys Jones and Miss Dora Musi for assistance in preparing visual or textual material; and to Scottie Wilson for some illuminating conversations.

Illustrations on pages 25, 28, 121, 132 reproduced by kind permission of Farbenfabriken Bayer AG, Leverkusen; on pages 81, 82, 89, 95, 96, 159 by kind permission of Galerie Rothe, Heidelberg. Photographs on pages 48, 124 by John Bignell; on pages 66, 67, 129 by Beryl Sokoloff; on pages 86, 130 by Dragoljub Kažić; on page 127 by Shunk-Kender; on pages 134, 148, 149, 157 by Maurice Olsen.

Index